DK

AN ANTHOLOGY OF
Fossils

WARNING: This book is an introduction to amazing fossils around the world, and is not a field guide to fossil hunting. If you choose to go fossil hunting, ensure you have permission to do so in the area and take all necessary safety precautions, some of which are outlined on page 122. The publisher cannot accept any liability for damage or injury that you may sustain as a result of fossil hunting activities.

AN ANTHOLOGY OF Fossils

Written by Dr Dean Lomax
Illustrated by Angela Rizza and Dilbag Singh

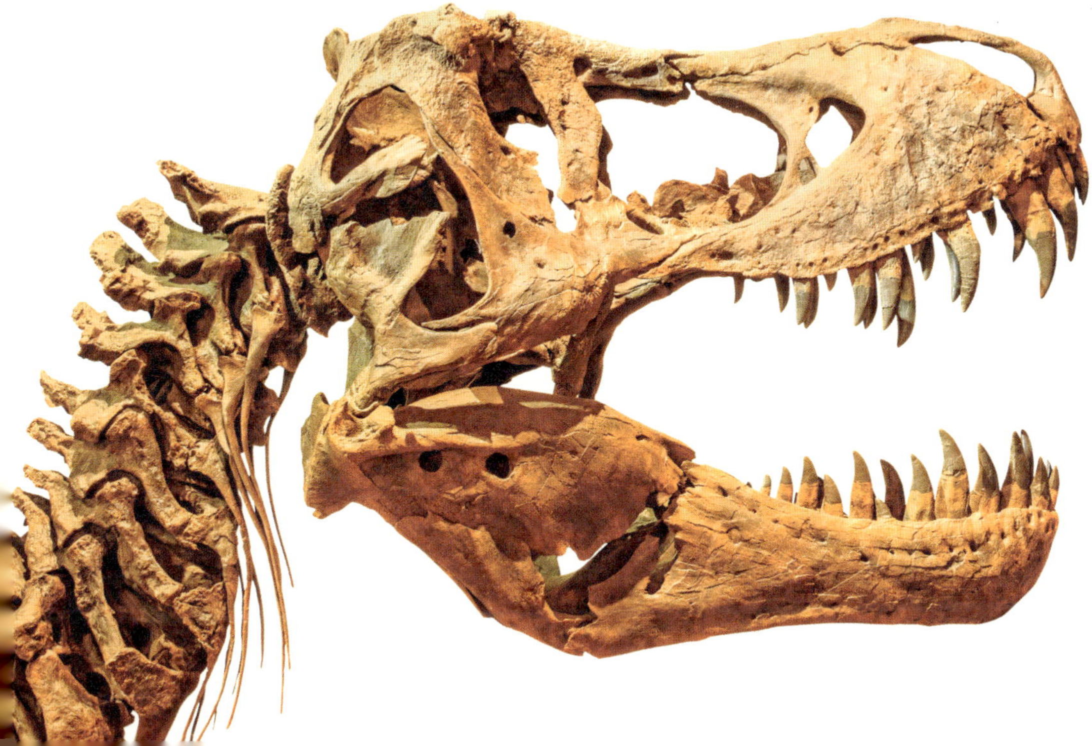

Contents

Making a fossil 6
Types of fossil 8
The age of fossils 10

PALEOZOIC ERA 12
Anomalocaris 13
Opabinia 14
Ottoia 15
Isotelus 16
Eurypterus 17
Pugnax 18
Aviculopecten 19
Halysites 20
Heliophyllum 21
Burgess Shale 22
Cantabrigiaster 24
Platyceras 25
Cooksonia 26
Alasemenia 27
Pecopteris 28
Lepidodendron 29
Didymograptus 30
Vaderlimulus 31
Meganeura 32
Arthropleura 33
Haikouichthys 34
Ngamugawi 35
Dunkleosteus 36
Helicoprion 37
Xenacanthus 38

Tiktaalik 39
Mastodonsaurus 40
Inostrancevia 41
Dimetrodon 42
Lystrosaurus 43

MESOZOIC ERA 44
Tyrannosaurus 45
Herrerasaurus 46
Arizonasaurus 47
Tanystropheus 48
Lisowicia 49
Ginkgo 50
Seirocrinus 51
Ichthyosaurus 52
Ichthyotitan 53
Record breakers 54
Leedsichthys 56
Cretapsara 57
Albertonectes 58
Kronosaurus 59
Hildoceras 60
Megateuthis 61
Cryolophosaurus 62
Proceratosaurus 63
Studying behaviour 64
Pterodaustro 66
Confuciusornis 67
Hesperornithoides 68
Supersaurus 69

Repenomamus	70
Maiasaura	71
Miragaia	72
Zuul	73
Archaeopteryx	74
Quetzalcoatlus	75
Xiphactinus	76
Tylosaurus	77
Araucaria	78
Magnolia	79
Lokiceratops	80
Parasaurolophus	81
Deinosuchus	82
Carnotaurus	83
Velociraptor	84
Spinosaurus	85
Triceratops	86
Pachycephalosaurus	87

CENOZOIC ERA 88

Woolly mammoth	89
Pakicetus	90
Basilosaurus	91
Icadyptes	92
Ceratogaulus	93
Paraceratherium	94
Titanoboa	95
Stupendemys	96
Darwinius	97
Famous fossil sites	*98*
Sifrhippus	100
Procoptodon	101
Icaronycteris	102
Titanomyrma	103
Platanus	104
Turritella	105
Borophagus	106
Archaeotherium	107
Gomphotherium	108
Mastodon	109
Phorusrhacos	110
Diplomystus	111
Rododelphis	112
Otodus megalodon	113
Doedicurus	114
Smilodon	115
Megatherium	116
Australopithecus	117
Fossil finders	*118*
A dinosaur dig	*120*
Can you find a fossil?	*122*
Glossary	124
Index	126
Acknowledgements	128

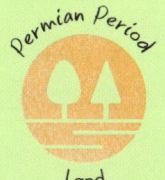

Look out for these pictures at the top of most pages. They will tell you what time period the plant or animal is from and where it lived.

Making a fossil

We only know that ancient animals and plants existed on our planet because of their fossils — the remains or traces of ancient life preserved in rocks. A scientist who studies fossils is called a paleontologist.

How do fossils form?

Fossilization is very rare. It depends on multiple factors — from how and where the animal died to whether it was buried quickly or eaten.

Of all the ancient animals and plants, only a small percentage might become fossils.

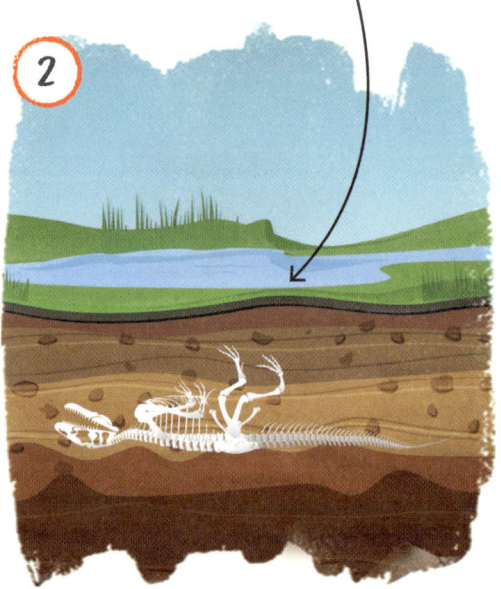

Death

After an animal dies, if it is not eaten or eroded (worn away by wind and rain), it may become a fossil. However, to help in this process, it must have died near or in water, where it may get buried by sediment.

Burial

As the remains are buried, usually only the hard parts, such as teeth or bones, are left. Sometimes, the soft parts may also be preserved. The body is then buried deeper, and more layers are added over the years.

More than just dinosaurs

Dinosaurs are the superstars of the prehistoric world. However, fossils provide snapshots of the entire history of life on Earth — from fossilized pollen to massive marine reptiles. They all contribute to our understanding of how life evolved (changed or developed over time).

A well-preserved fossil flower

Becoming rock
The skeleton and soft parts are slowly replaced by minerals from the surrounding sediment. These minerals gradually seep into the bones, changing them into rock. The body is now fossilized, inside a layer of rock.

Discovery
Millions of years later, the layers of rock above the fossil erode to reveal the remains. This might be discovered by a fossil hunter who reports it to a museum.

Types of fossil

Fossils come in all shapes and sizes. There are two main types — body fossils that preserve the hard parts of a creature or plant, and trace fossils that are evidence of their activities. Body fossils include bones, shells, and leaves, while trace fossils can be in the form of nests, tracks, and fossilized poo (coprolites).

Skeletons

Fossilized skeletons are the most famous body fossils. The remains of bones and teeth are direct evidence of life forms. Sometimes, even the most delicate parts of the skeleton can reveal fascinating details, but finding a fully complete skeleton is rare.

The skeleton of a Stegoceras is a good example of a body fossil.

This dinosaur walked on two legs.

Amber

Ancient creatures were sometimes trapped inside sticky tree resin that hardened and formed amber. This unusual form of fossilization often captured those animals and plants in incredible detail. Sometimes, both body and trace fossils were preserved together.

A prehistoric fly in amber

Fossil footprints are one of the most common trace fossils.

Tracks

Tracks or footprints are well-known trace fossils. These record a moment in time. By studying tracks, we may discover how fast an animal moved, whether it was part of a herd, or even if it was digging.

Baby mammoth frozen in permafrost

Frozen in time

Many Ice Age animals have been found frozen in permafrost (completely frozen ground). These creatures include woolly mammoths, woolly rhinos, cave lions, wolves, and bison. The remains are often in superb condition and may even preserve organs.

The age of fossils

The Earth is about 4.5 billion years old. Scientists divide the age of the Earth into big chunks called eras, which are further divided into shorter periods. These indicate how life changed on our planet. There are three major eras of time – the Paleozoic, Mesozoic, and Cenozoic.

Oldest fossils

The evidence of earliest life on Earth was revealed by the fossils of single-celled, tiny organisms called bacteria. These fossils are a staggering 3.5 billion years old.

A paleontologist studying a fossil.

This stromatolite fossil is about 2.7 billion years old.

How do we date fossils?

Scientists use a technique called radiometric dating to carefully study the rate of decay of radioactive elements, such as potassium, inside rocks. This helps them to identify the age of rocks and the fossils found in them.

Animals and plants

The rocky remains of fossils tell us that the first animals and plants appeared more than half a billion years ago. Fossils are Earth's memories of the past and provide incredible evidence of lost worlds.

A skeleton of a Parasaurolophus that lived 75 million years ago (MYA).

Although very small, Spriggina was among the first larger animals to appear.

A time of slime

Some of the oldest fossils are stromatolites. They were formed as tiny bacteria grew between layers of sand and mud, which built up over time and created mounds of slime.

Some stromatolites exist today, such as this one in Hamelin Bay, Australia.

Spectacular finds

For a long time, only single-celled life existed. But amazing discoveries like those in the Ediacara Hills, Australia, showed remains of early multicellular organisms, such as Spriggina.

11

Paleozoic Era

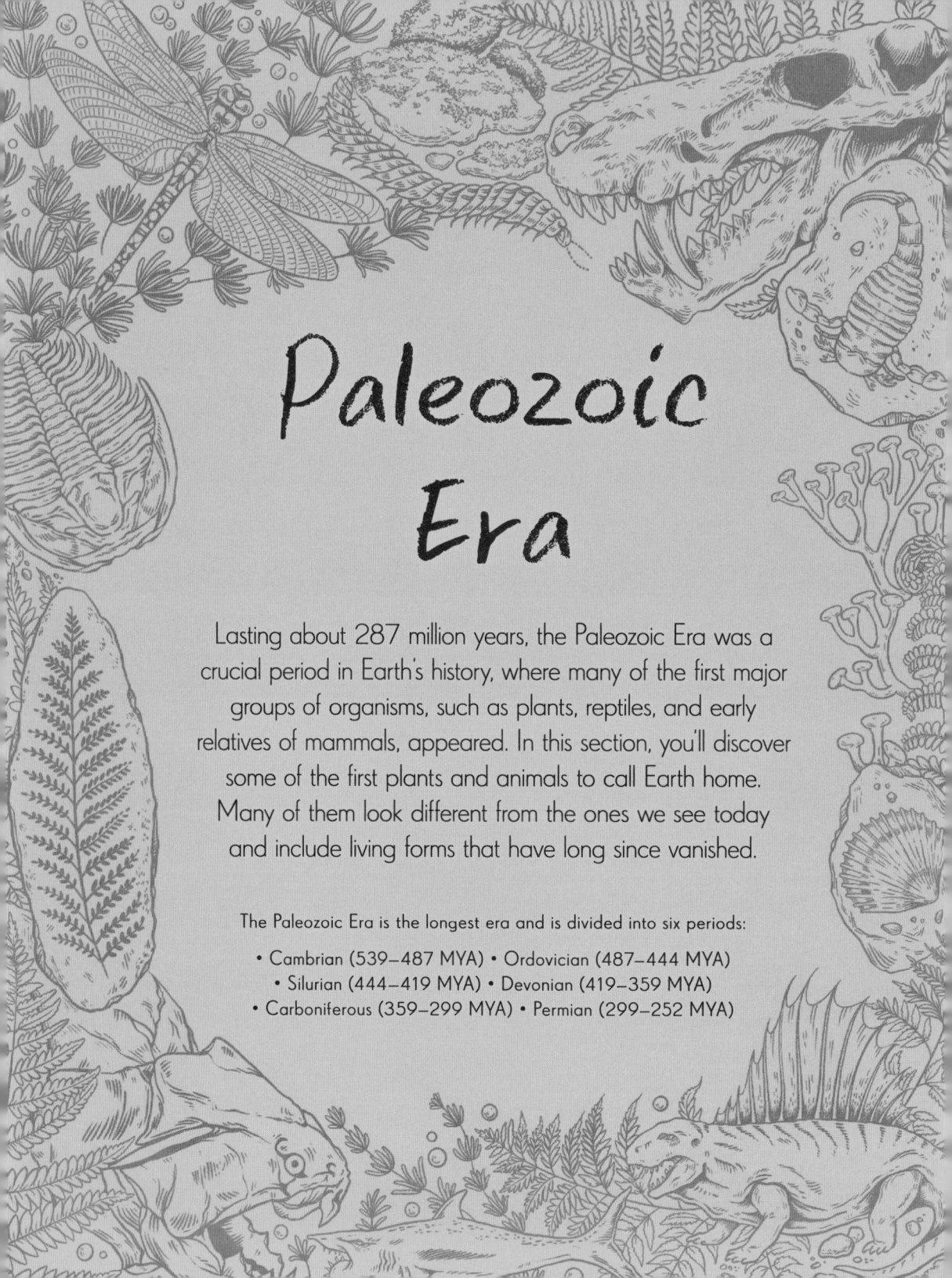

Lasting about 287 million years, the Paleozoic Era was a crucial period in Earth's history, where many of the first major groups of organisms, such as plants, reptiles, and early relatives of mammals, appeared. In this section, you'll discover some of the first plants and animals to call Earth home. Many of them look different from the ones we see today and include living forms that have long since vanished.

The Paleozoic Era is the longest era and is divided into six periods:
- Cambrian (539–487 MYA) • Ordovician (487–444 MYA)
- Silurian (444–419 MYA) • Devonian (419–359 MYA)
- Carboniferous (359–299 MYA) • Permian (299–252 MYA)

Anomalocaris
a-NOM-a-low-CAR-iss

Anomalocaris was one of the first super predators on Earth. This unusual animal used its large mouthparts and excellent vision to snatch prey. It had a circular mouth with tooth-like structures. The first fossils were discovered in the Burgess Shale, a famous fossil site in Canada.

Notes

- Anomalocaris had a body length of up to 1 m (3 ft).
- More fossils have been found in Australia, China, and the USA.
- The first fossils were described in 1892.

Anomalocaris had two large mouthparts at the front, like this one.

Cambrian Period — Water

This shows only a part of the animal's body.

Cambrian Period
Water

This early predator had a body length of about 8 cm (3 in).

The proboscis had a claw that was probably used to pick up soft prey, such as fish, from the seabed.

Its pairs of overlapping flaps along the sides helped it swim.

Opabinia

OH-pa-BIN-ee-a

One of the strangest of all the Cambrian creatures is Opabinia. With five eyes, a long, flexible mouthpart or proboscis, and an unusual body, this animal seems alien-like. Paleontologists agree that it is a type of early arthropod (an animal with a hard outer skeleton and a body made of jointed parts, such as a woodlouse).

Ottoia

ot-OY-ah

This animal belonged to a group of worms, called priapulids. Ottoia was one of the top predators of its time. It lived on the muddy seabed, hiding inside burrows. Sitting in wait, Ottoia was probably an ambush predator and would snatch prey that came too close.

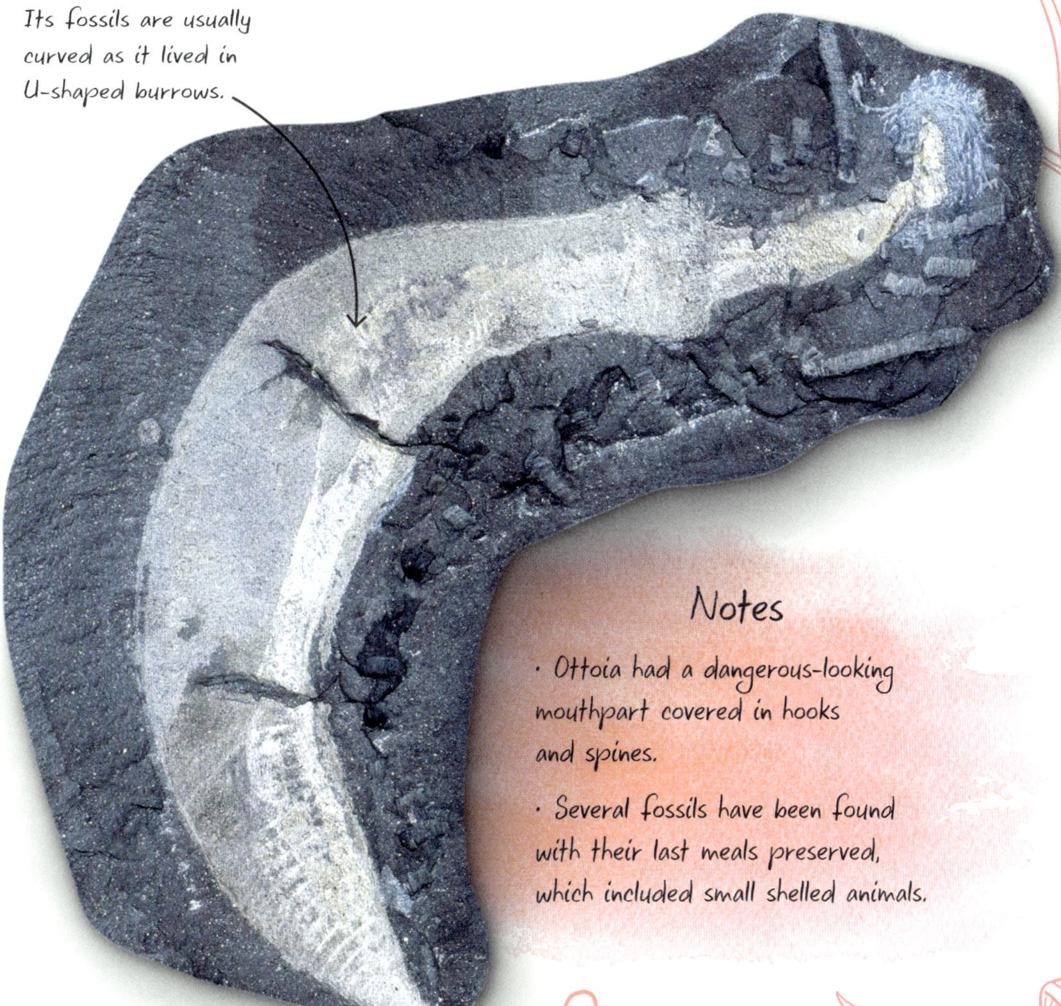

Cambrian Period

Water

Its fossils are usually curved as it lived in U-shaped burrows.

Notes

- Ottoia had a dangerous-looking mouthpart covered in hooks and spines.

- Several fossils have been found with their last meals preserved, which included small shelled animals.

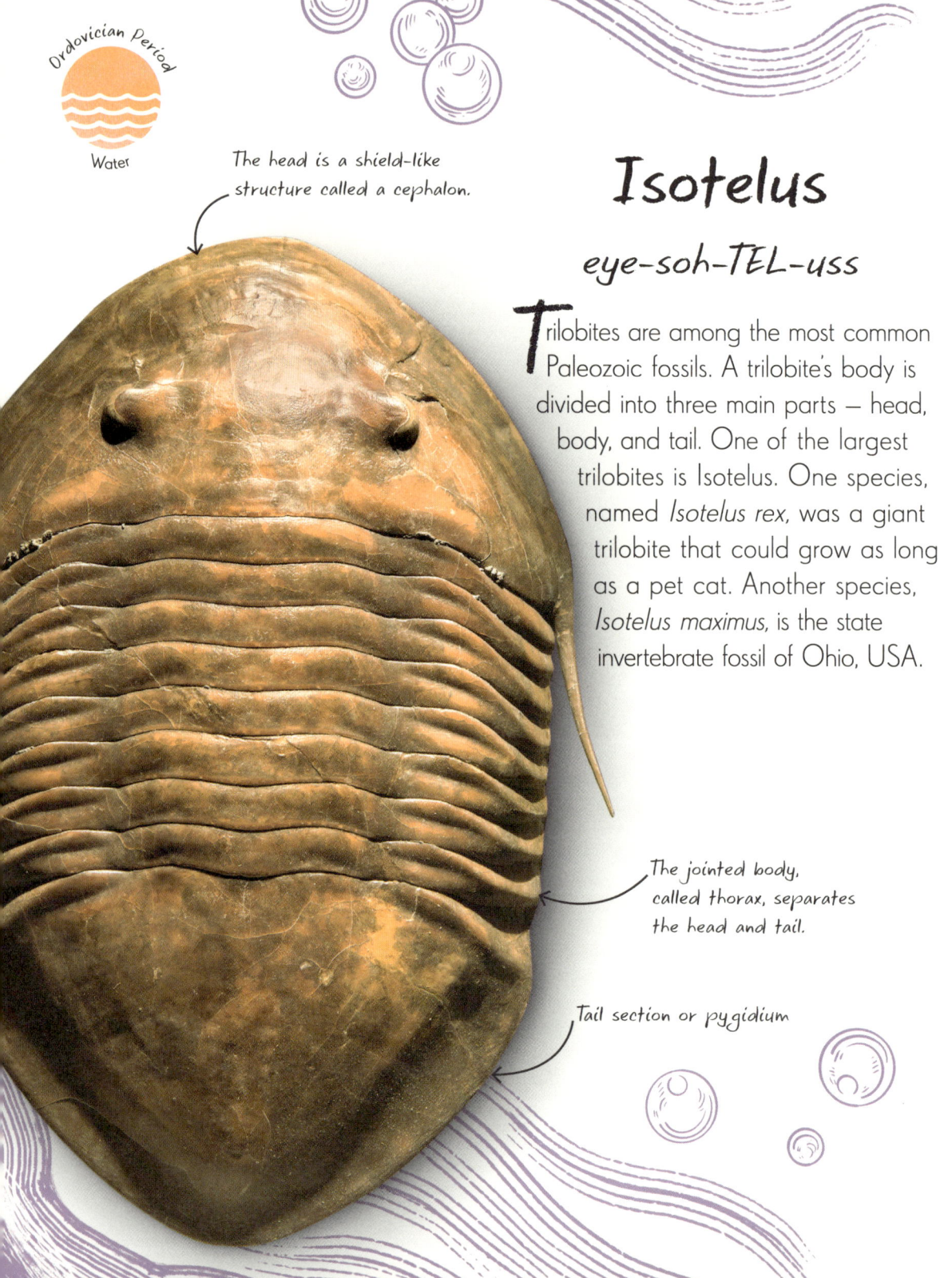

Ordovician Period
Water

The head is a shield-like structure called a cephalon.

Isotelus

eye-soh-TEL-uss

Trilobites are among the most common Paleozoic fossils. A trilobite's body is divided into three main parts — head, body, and tail. One of the largest trilobites is Isotelus. One species, named *Isotelus rex*, was a giant trilobite that could grow as long as a pet cat. Another species, *Isotelus maximus*, is the state invertebrate fossil of Ohio, USA.

The jointed body, called thorax, separates the head and tail.

Tail section or pygidium

Its paddle-like legs were used to push itself through the water.

Eurypterus had a spikelike tail spine.

Silurian Period
Water

Eurypterus

you-RIP-teh-russ

This ancient creature gives its name to a group of animals called eurypterids or sea scorpions. Eurypterus is the most common type of eurypterids. The members of this group looked a bit like modern scorpions, but did not have a venomous stinger.

Notes

- Eurypterus fossils have been found in Europe and North America.
- It was named in 1825.
- One eurypterid, named Jaekelopterus, was about 2.6 m (9 ft) long and is the largest known sea scorpion.

Devonian-Permian Periods
Water

Pugnax
PUG-nacks

Pugnax was a very common type of brachiopod, a group of shelled sea creatures. Like all brachiopods, Pugnax was a soft-bodied animal that lived inside a hard shell and attached itself to the seafloor using a fleshy stalk. Brachiopods were especially common during the Paleozoic, but many became extinct at the end of the Permian.

Brachiopods filter tiny plants and animals, called plankton, from water before feeding on them.

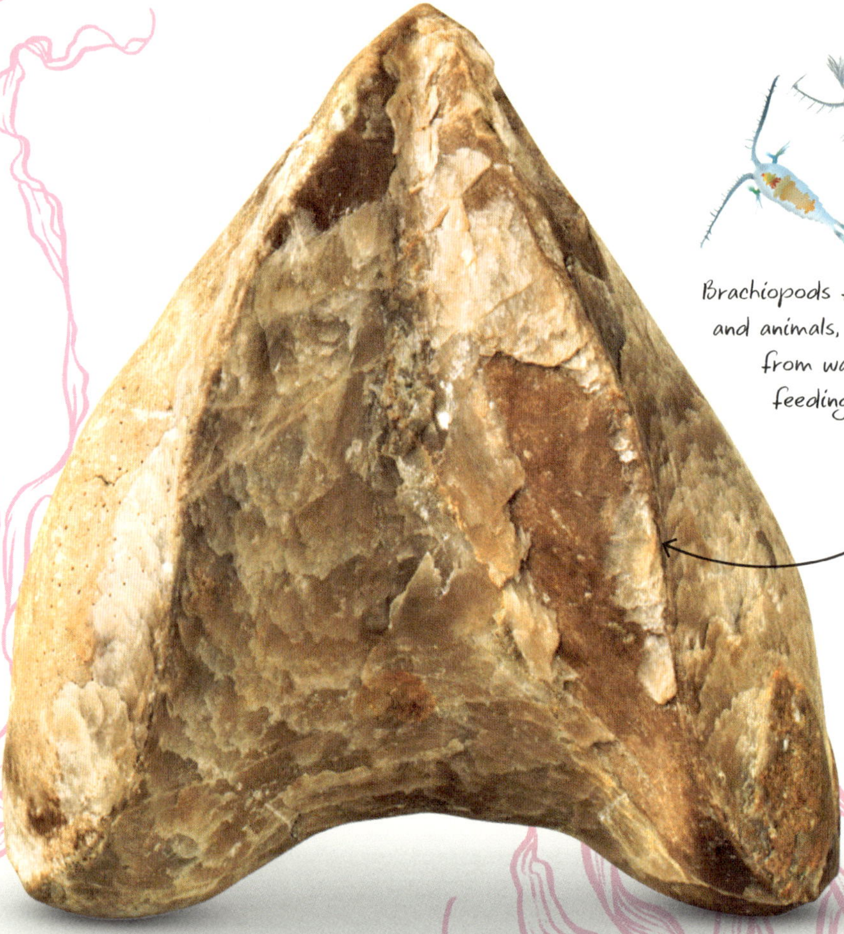

Outlines with distinct ridges (raised areas)

The zigzag pattern helped it blend in with its surroundings.

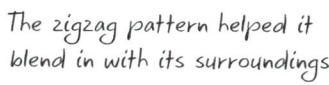
Devonian-Triassic Periods
Water

Notes

• Aviculopecten is a type of bivalve mollusc, the same group that includes oysters and clams.

• The first bivalves appeared more than 500 million years ago.

• Some fossilized bivalves have been found with pearls inside.

The hinge at this end allowed the animal to open its shell and extend its tentacles to trap tiny organisms for food.

Aviculopecten
a-vik-yoo-loh-PEK-ten

Many bivalves, such as Aviculopecten, look similar to brachiopods and are often mistaken for them. Bivalves, however, are a type of mollusc with a two-piece shell (or valve) joined together. A quick way of telling their fossils apart is by looking at the two valves of a bivalve, which are mirror images of each other.

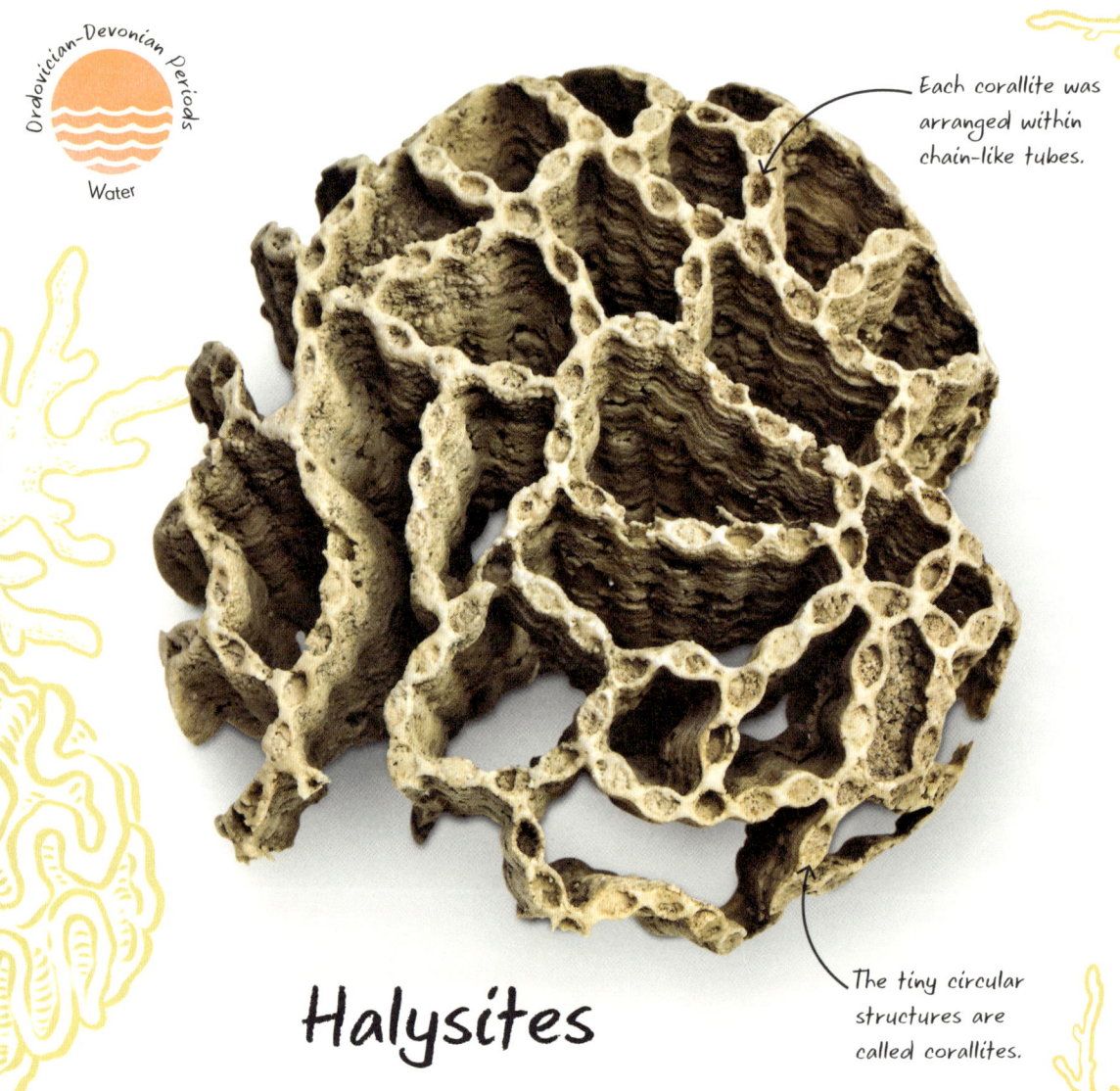

Ordovician-Devonian Periods — Water

Each corallite was arranged within chain-like tubes.

The tiny circular structures are called corallites.

Halysites

hal-EE-sy-TEES

This chain-like structure is an ancient species of coral. Halysites is a famous fossil chain coral that lived in large colonies in warm, shallow waters and reefs. Like modern coral reefs, many animals made their homes in and around these ancient reefs. Halysites fossils have been found worldwide.

Heliophyllum

he-LEO-fy-lum

Devonian Period
Water

Heliophyllum is an extinct type of coral that lived inside a rocky skeleton fixed to the seabed. Studies have shown that it added a thin layer to its skeleton each day. It is nicknamed "horn coral" due to the fossil's hornlike shape. Its fossils are often found together in large numbers.

The bottom end would have stuck to the seafloor.

Notes

- Heliophyllum was named in 1846.

- It is among the most common Devonian corals and is found worldwide.

- Its long, stinging tentacles helped to catch tiny prey.

Burgess Shale

Situated high in the Canadian Rockies in British Columbia, Canada, Burgess Shale is one of the most important fossil sites. It was found in 1909 by paleontologist Charles Doolittle Walcott. The discovery changed our understanding of early life during the Cambrian Period, around 508 million years ago.

Charles Doolittle Walcott (1850-1927)

A trilobite fossil discovered at this site.

Amazing fossils

Walcott collected around 65,000 fossils, including some of the more famous but rare ones. However, today, almost 200 different species have been found and identified at this fossil site.

Paleontologists looking for new fossils at Burgess Shale

Ancient environment

The Burgess Shale records a rich environment of marine animals that lived together on a muddy seabed. The fossils are so well preserved that even soft parts, such as internal organs, can still be seen.

Some fossils show its tiny head.

Wiwaxia

This mysterious, slug-like animal had rows of armour-like plates and long spines, which probably served as protection. Paleontologists have found that adults grew to about 5.5 cm (2 in) in length.

Long spines

Hallucigenia

This unusual creature has puzzled scientists since it was first discovered. In fact, during the 1970s, the spines along its back were mistaken for legs and its head was thought to be its tail. Only recently, scientists have figured out the correct order of its body parts.

Mountain by name

Walcott named many fossils from the Burgess Shale, including a small, shrimp-like creature. He called it *Waptia fieldensis* after two mountains near the fossil site — Mount Wapta and Mount Field.

Mount Wapta

Cantabrigiaster
can-TA-brig-ee-AS-ter

Cantabrigiaster is one of the earliest sea star-like animals, perhaps the first ancestor of the sea star family. It lived in an ancient cold-water reef more than 480 million years ago. This detailed fossil was found in Morocco, Africa, and studied in 2021. It was an important discovery as it helped scientists to understand how echinoderms evolved.

Notes

- Sea stars are part of a group of animals called echinoderms, which also includes brittle stars and sea urchins.
- Cold-water reefs are structures found in deeper, darker parts of the ocean.

Like most sea stars, Cantabrigiaster had five arms.

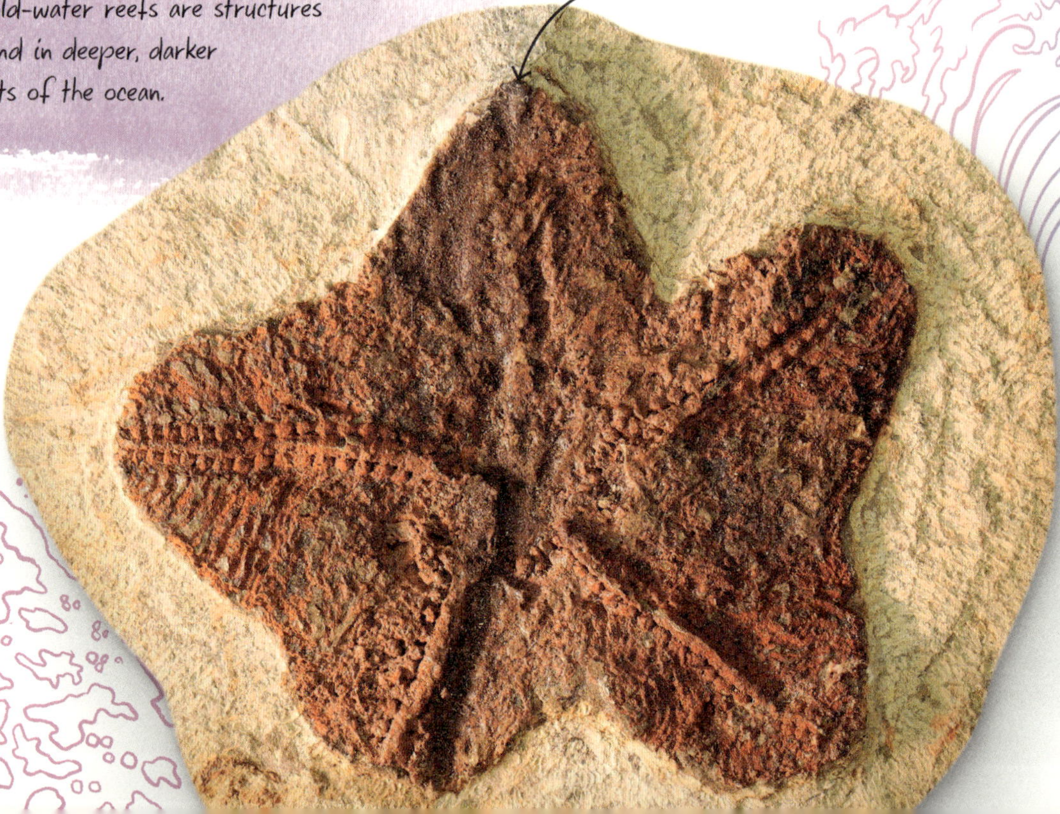

Its typical length was 4 cm (1.5 in).

Its shell was spiralled but flattened.

Silurian-Carboniferous Periods
Water

The first few whorls (coils) are loosely spiralled.

Platyceras

plat-ee-SAIR-as

These early types of gastropod snails have a cap-like shell. The curved shells are found worldwide and were especially abundant throughout the Silurian to the Carboniferous Periods. In an unusual discovery, some fossils of crinoids (a type of echinoderms) have been found infested with Platyceras that were feeding on the crinoid's poo! This behaviour is known as coprophagy.

The gastropods are the largest group of molluscs, which include snails and slugs.

25

Cooksonia

cook-SOH-nee-a

Cooksonia was among the earliest land plants. One of the unique features of this plant was its Y-shaped branches. The plants usually had one to two branches, but some had as many as six. Its fossils are found in rocks that are more than 400 million years old. The first fossils were found inside a quarry in Wales, UK.

Silurian-Devonian Periods — Land

Its length was usually 6 cm (2 in).

Sturdy stem held the plant upright

Notes

- Cooksonia had no leaves, flowers, or roots.
- Each branch had an oval-shaped bag called a sporangium, which contained spores. Like seeds, spores can grow into new plants.

Devonian Period
Land

Winged samaras, also known as "helicopter seeds", spread their seeds with the help of wind, just like Alasemenia did millions of years ago.

Alasemenia

al-as-ME-ne-ah

Alasemenia was discovered inside a mine in China in 2024. It is one of the earliest known examples of a winged seed and is 365 million years old. This seed had wing-like structures that helped it glide in the wind. Its fossils provide new details about how ancient seeds developed and spread to grow new plants.

Its typical length was 2.5-3.3 cm (1-1.3 in).

Carboniferous-Permian Periods — Land

Pecopteris
peh-KOP-teh-riss

Pecopteris is the name for the leaves of several trees, such as Psaronius, which were common during the Carboniferous. This period is often called the "Age of Plants", as many new types appeared and spread across the globe. Most Psaronius fossils are isolated leaves, such as Pecopteris, and branches, often preserving fine details.

Each leaf was divided into leaflets.

In life, the many leaves of Pecopteris would have looked like those of a palm tree.

The typical leaf length was 25 cm (10 in).

28

Lepidodendron

leh-pi-doh-DEN-dron

One of the first giant plants, Lepidodendron formed vast tropical forests surrounding watery swamps. Most of their fossils are large chunks of bark with a diamond-like pattern, formed when the leaves fell off. For this reason, Lepidodendron is sometimes known as the "scale tree".

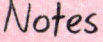

Carboniferous-Permian Periods
Land

Scale-like bark

Notes

- Lepidodendron was home to many early animals.

- Plants like Lepidodendron formed most of the world's coal.

- Nestled inside one rare giant scale tree were the remains of an adult and a young Dendromaia, an early lizard-like creature.

Reached heights of around 30 m (98 ft)

Ordovician Period
Water

Notes

• Didymograptus had a two-pronged shape that resembled a tuning fork. Hence, it is often called the "tuning fork graptolite".

• The name graptolite means "written rock" as many of its fossils resemble rock carvings.

Didymograptus
did-ee-moh-GRAP-tuss

Though it might look a bit like a plant, the odd-looking Didymograptus was a graptolite — a type of marine animal that lived in colonies. The fossil is made up of small colonies formed by tiny animals called zooids. These lived and floated along in the sea, where they fed on microscopic plankton.

The zooids lived inside these tooth-like structures.

Vaderlimulus
vay-duh-LIM-you-luss

When its discovery was announced in 2017, Vaderlimulus was the only known horseshoe crab from the Triassic of North America. Scientists named it after its head shield that resembled the helmet of Darth Vader from *Star Wars*. There are only four living species of horseshoe crabs today, but ancient species like Vaderlimulus had many different features.

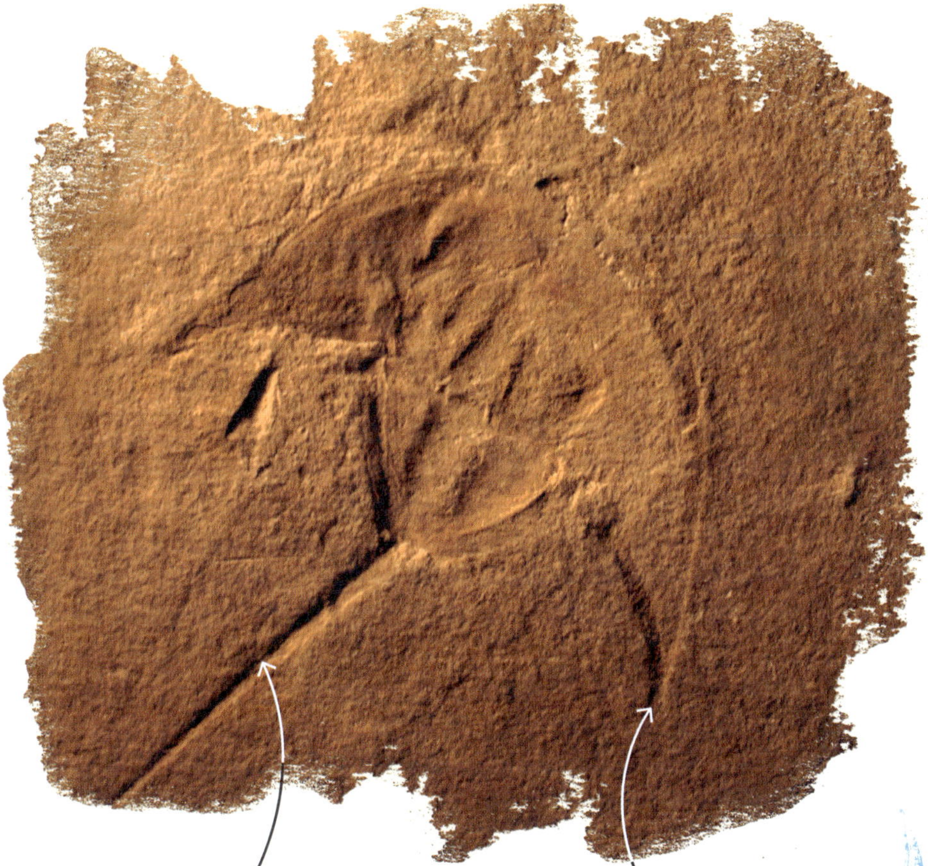

The spinelike tail is called a telson.

Its typical length was 10 cm (4 in).

Carboniferous Period

Land

Air

Wingspan of at least 70 cm (26 in), about as wide as a common kestrel

Most Meganeura fossils show detailed veins in the wings.

Meganeura

MEGA-new-ra

About the same size as a large pigeon, Meganeura was a giant flying insect related to dragonflies. It had four broad wings that could move independently. Each wing was attached to its long body by a hinge. Meganeura was a fast flier with the ability to change its position and direction quickly.

Notes

- Although Meganeura hunted insects, it may also have caught tiny reptiles and amphibians.

- It was among the largest flying insects ever to have lived.

- Meganeura is also called griffenfly.

Arthropleura's body was divided into about 30 jointed parts.

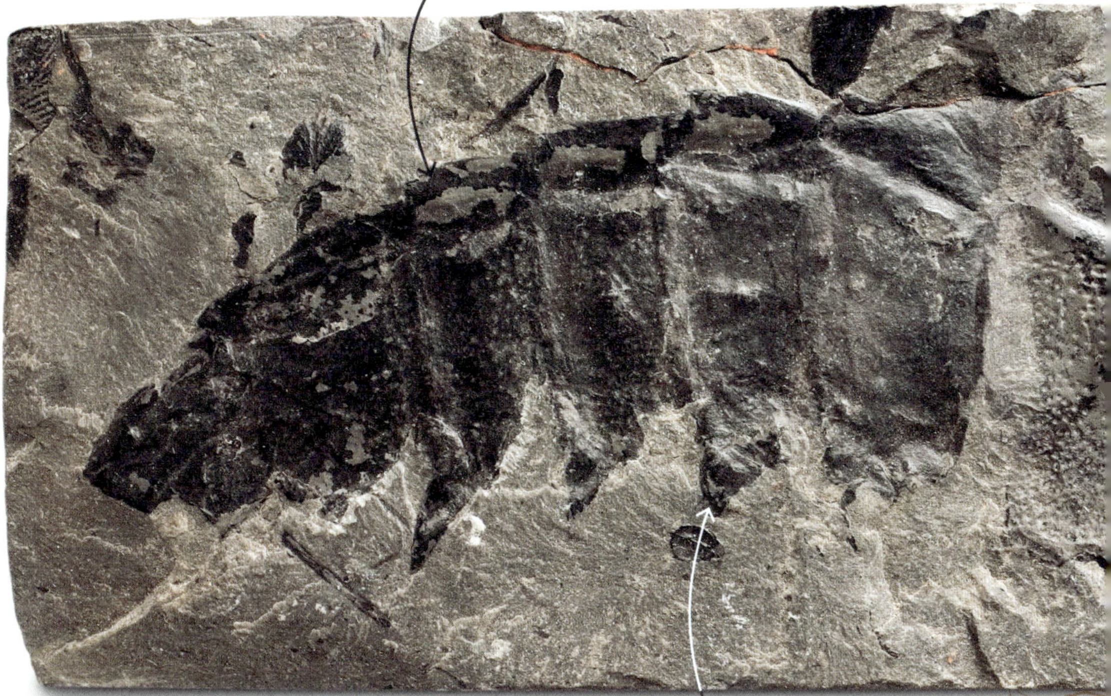

It may have had as many as 120 legs.

Arthropleura

arth-row-PLOO-ra

Considered the largest arthropod of all time, Arthropleura was an enormous millipede that may have weighed about 50 kg (110 lb). Its fossils have been found in Europe and North America, and were first identified over 170 years ago. Most fossils are isolated parts of the body. However, very rarely, more complete ones have also been found.

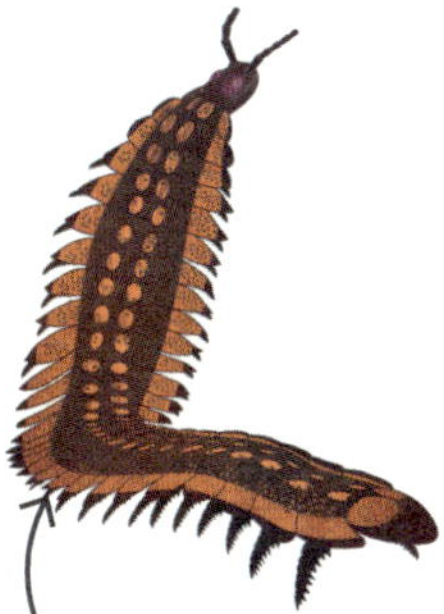

It grew to about 260 cm (8.5 ft) long, much taller than an average human being.

Cambrian Period
Water

Haikouichthys

HIGH-koo-ICK-thiss

It might be difficult to imagine, but for a long time, there were no fish in the world's oceans. Haikouichthys might be one of the earliest fish or fish-like creatures, appearing around 518 million years ago. It was also one of the first animals with a backbone. It had a very small head with two tiny eyes, no jaws or teeth, and undeveloped gills and fins.

Notes

- More than 500 fossils have been found at Chengjiang in Yunnan Province, China.

- Haikouichthys was named after the city of Haikou in China. The name means "fish from Haikou".

- Haikouichthys was only about 2.5 cm (1 in) long.

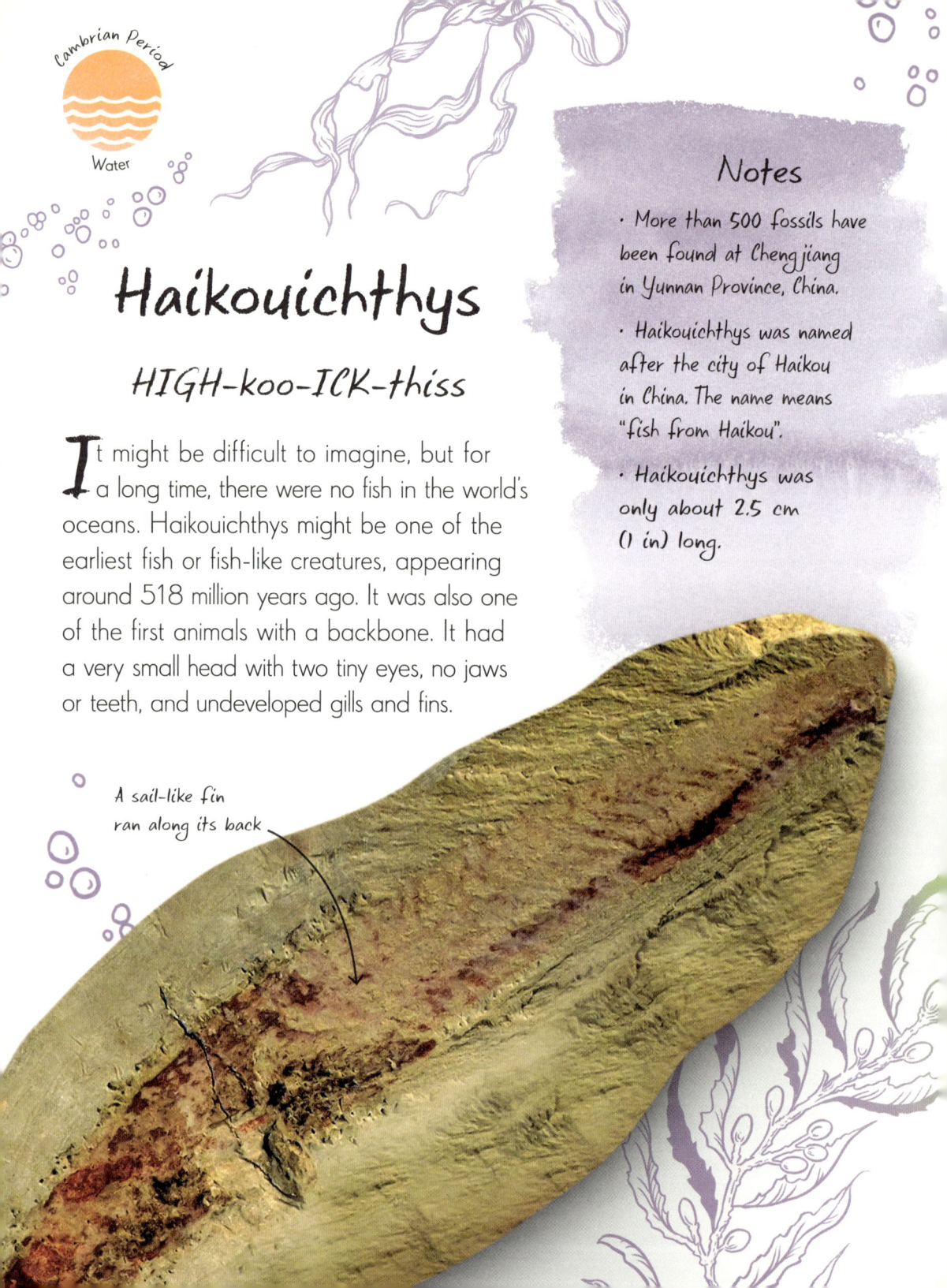

A sail-like fin ran along its back

Devonian Period

Water

The fossil shows the skull with many individual bones.

Ngamugawi

na-moo-GA-we

Ngamugawi was a type of coelacanth, a fish with limb-like, fleshy fins. The fins were attached to its shoulder and hip. This group of fish played an important role in understanding how animals with a backbone, or vertebrates, developed over time.

There are only two living species of coelacanth. This West Indian Ocean coelacanth is one of them.

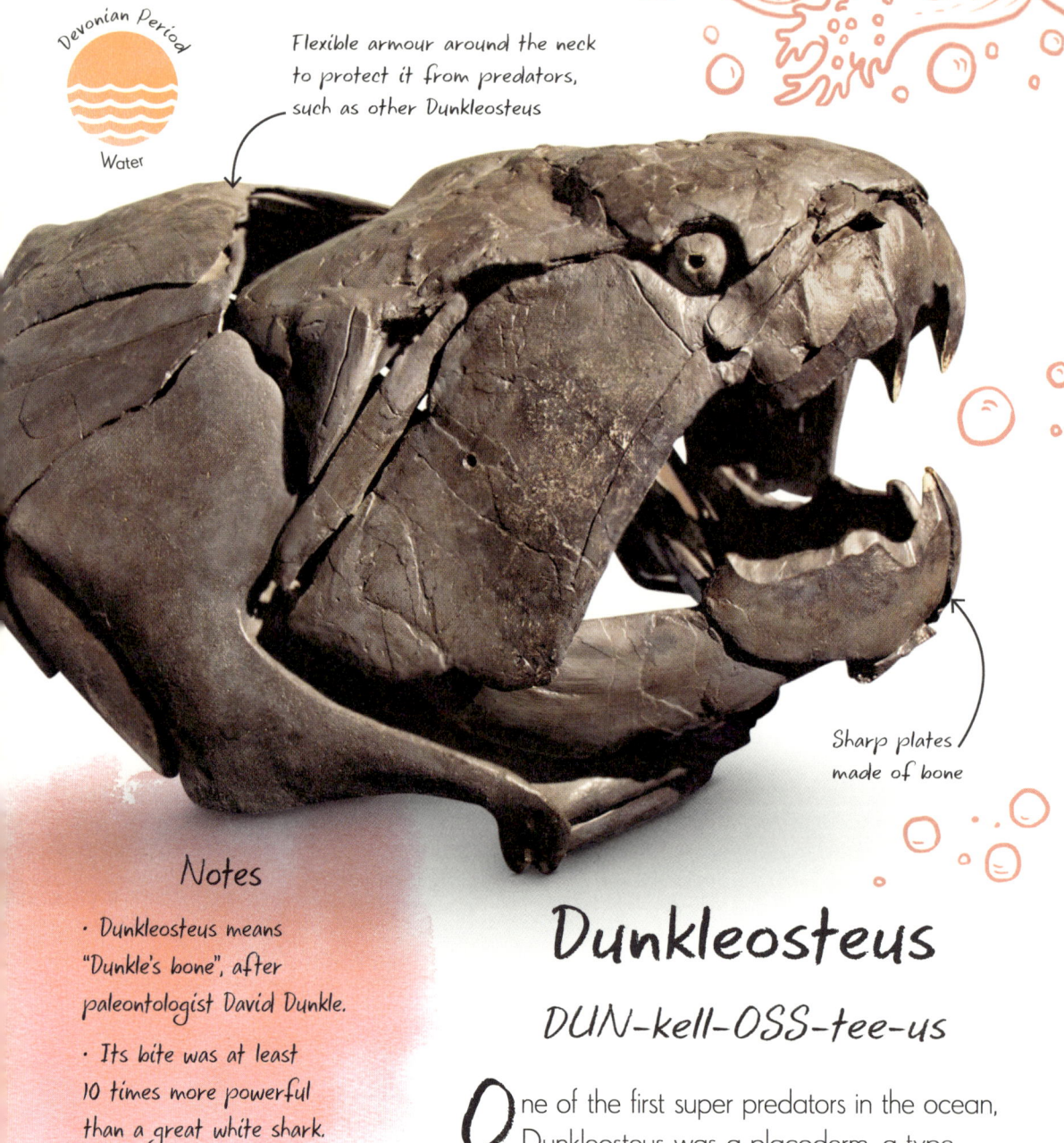

Devonian Period — Water

Flexible armour around the neck to protect it from predators, such as other Dunkleosteus

Sharp plates made of bone

Notes

- Dunkleosteus means "Dunkle's bone", after paleontologist David Dunkle.
- Its bite was at least 10 times more powerful than a great white shark.

Dunkleosteus

DUN-kell-OSS-tee-us

One of the first super predators in the ocean, Dunkleosteus was a placoderm, a type of armoured fish. Placoderms were among the earliest fish to evolve jaws. However, instead of teeth, Dunkleosteus had thick, self-sharpening and fang-like bony plates that sliced through its prey.

Helicoprion

HELL-ee-coe-PRY-on

Permian Period

Water

Helicoprion was a bizarre, shark-like fish related to a group of living fish called chimaeras or ratfish. Helicoprion fossils have a spiral-shaped cluster of teeth, called a tooth whorl, which was set into the lower jaw. Unlike sharks, Helicoprion teeth never fell out.

The tooth whorls resembled the blades of a chainsaw.

Its front teeth hooked and sliced prey, the middle ones helped cut and tear, and the back teeth pushed the prey into its mouth.

Carboniferous-Triassic periods — Water

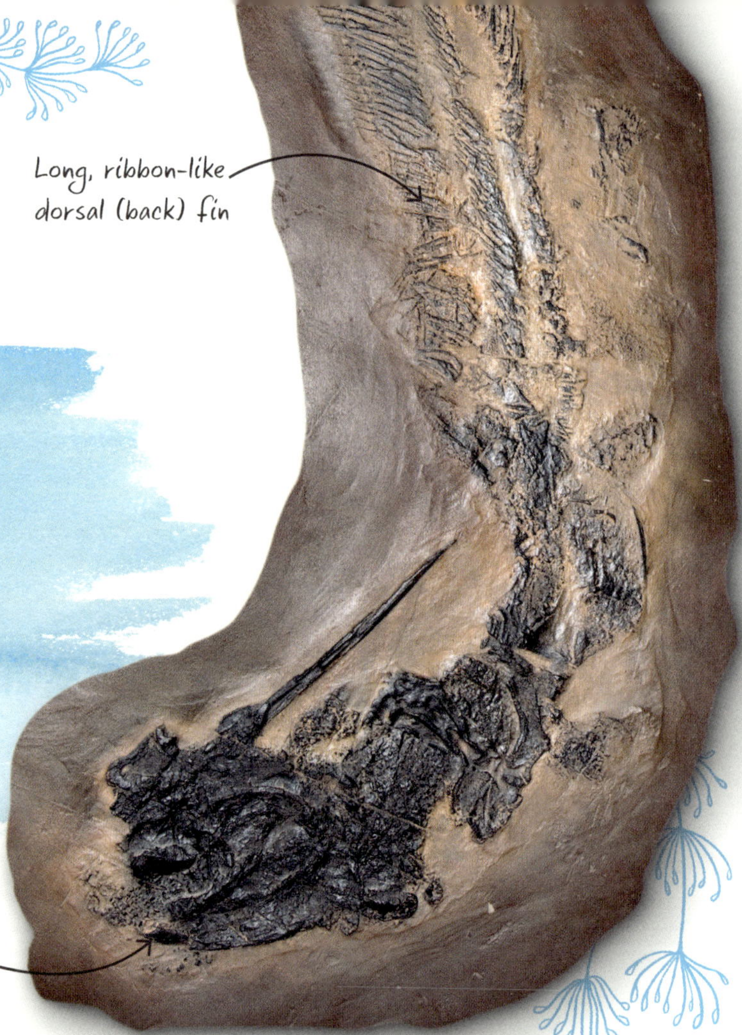

Long, ribbon-like dorsal (back) fin

Notes

- Xenacanthus means "foreign spine" in Greek, and is named after its unusual head spine.
- Its spine might have been used to attract mates.
- It had v-shaped teeth in its mouth and probably fed on fish.

Body length was 1-2 m (3-7 ft)

Xenacanthus
ZEE-nah-CAN-thus

Xenacanthus is an extinct type of freshwater shark that lived till the end of the Triassic. Its fossils have been found worldwide, and often include isolated teeth and fin spines. However, some exceptionally rare fossils from Europe have been found fully preserved with soft tissues, and even show a full body outline of this early shark.

Tiktaalik
tik-TAH-lik

Devonian Period
Water

Land

One of the first fish with limb-like fins, Tiktaalik evolved during the Devonian Period. Although this fish lived in freshwater lakes and rivers, it used its limb-like fins to drag itself out onto land. Tiktaalik had features of ancient fish and tetrapods (four-limbed animals), so it is often nicknamed a "fishapod". Its first fossils were unearthed during a trip to Arctic Canada in 2004.

Its body was covered with square-like, overlapping scales.

Flat and pointed skull

Over millions of years, the fin bones developed into limbs with fingers and toes, allowing them to take their first steps on land.

39

Triassic Period — Water, Land

Mastodonsaurus
MASS-toe-don-SORE-us

Reaching a size of up to 6 m (20 ft) long, Mastodonsaurus was one of the largest amphibians ever to have existed. This giant mostly lived in water and was probably one of the top predators of its time. Many fossils have been found in Europe, especially in southern Germany.

Its large, triangle-shaped skull could reach up to 1 m (3 ft) in length.

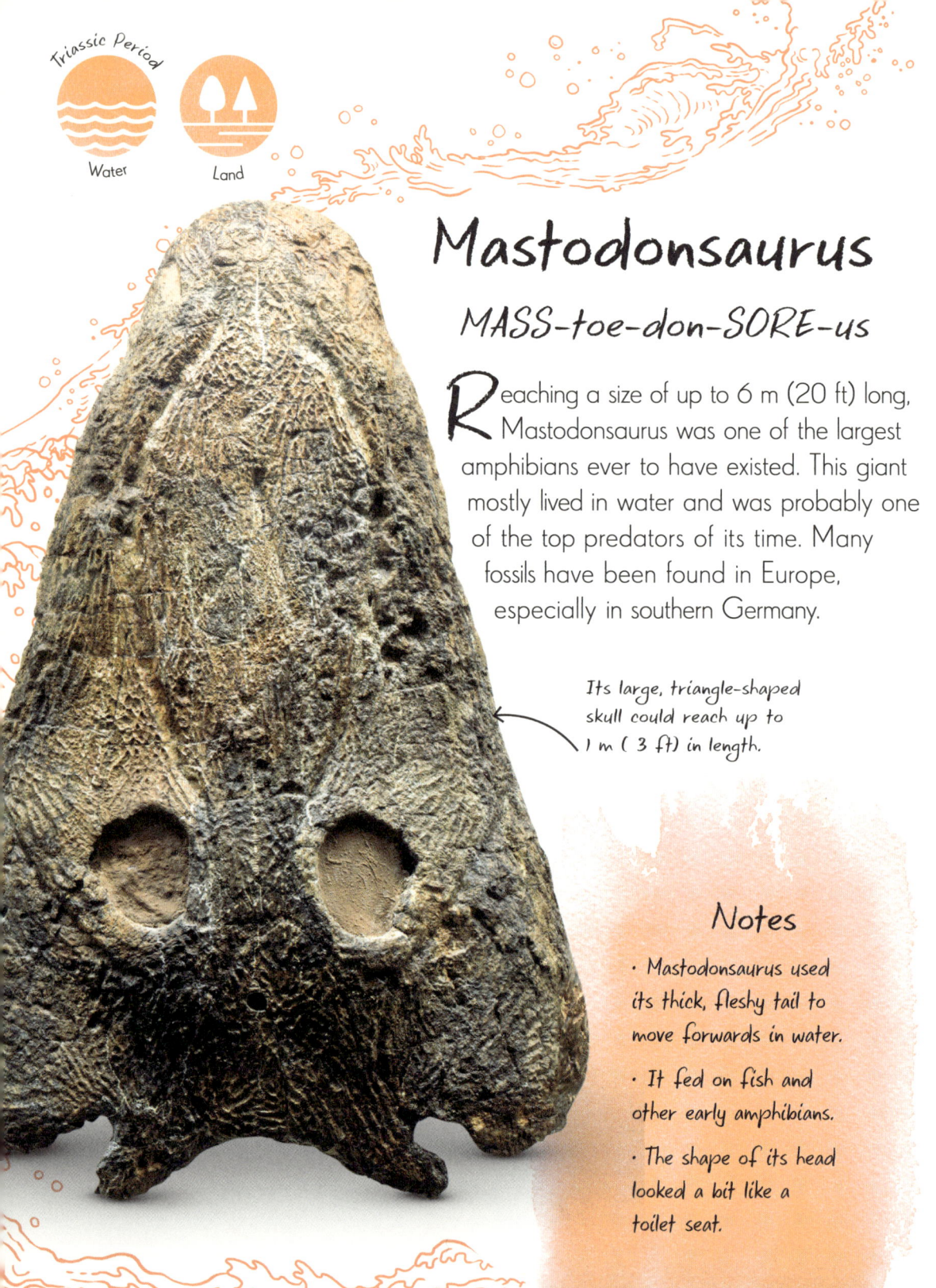

Notes

- Mastodonsaurus used its thick, fleshy tail to move forwards in water.
- It fed on fish and other early amphibians.
- The shape of its head looked a bit like a toilet seat.

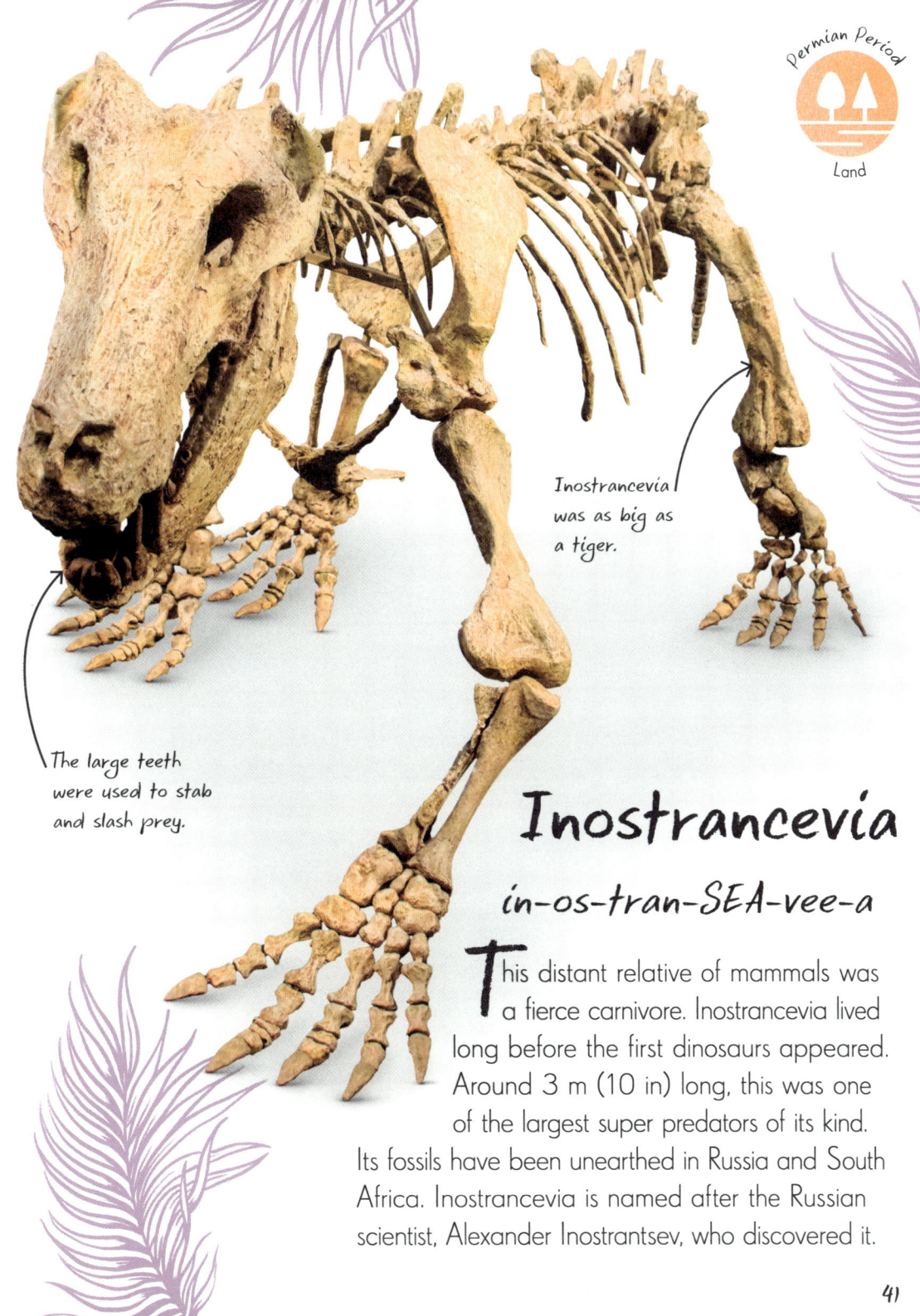

Permian Period

Land

Inostrancevia was as big as a tiger.

The large teeth were used to stab and slash prey.

Inostrancevia

in-os-tran-SEA-vee-a

This distant relative of mammals was a fierce carnivore. Inostrancevia lived long before the first dinosaurs appeared. Around 3 m (10 in) long, this was one of the largest super predators of its kind. Its fossils have been unearthed in Russia and South Africa. Inostrancevia is named after the Russian scientist, Alexander Inostrantsev, who discovered it.

Permian Period — Land

Large sail on its back

Notes
- The name Dimetrodon means "two measures of teeth" after the different types of teeth in its jaws.
- Its sail was used to attract mates and scare away predators.

It had sharp teeth and powerful jaws.

Dimetrodon
die-MET-roe-don

Often mistaken for a dinosaur, Dimetrodon lived millions of years before the first dinosaurs appeared. Measuring more than 4 m (13 ft) in length, it was one of the largest and earliest land predators ever to have walked on Earth. Dimetrodon fossils have been found in Europe and North America.

Lystrosaurus

LIS-trow-SORE-us

Permian-Triassic Periods
Land

This dog-sized herbivore lived about 250 million years ago, during the Late Permian to Early Triassic Periods. Fossils of several species of Lystrosaurus have been found across the globe. This was an important discovery as its fossils show that it survived the Permo–Triassic extinction, one of Earth's most devastating mass extinction events.

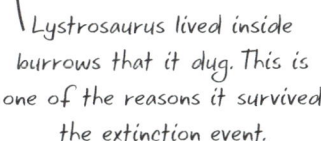

Lystrosaurus lived inside burrows that it dug. This is one of the reasons it survived the extinction event.

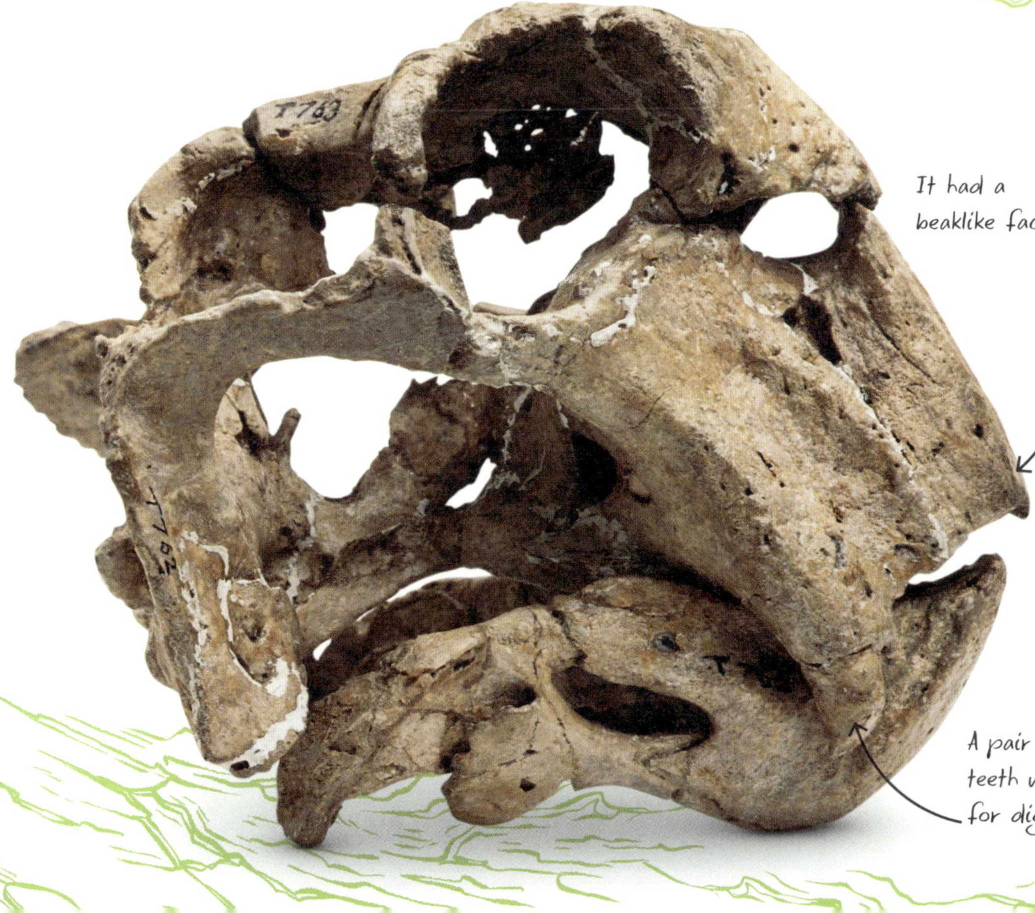

It had a beaklike face.

A pair of tusk-like teeth were used for digging.

Mesozoic Era

The Mesozoic Era is the most famous time in Earth's history. This is when the first dinosaurs appeared, and spread far and wide to conquer the planet. Many other groups of organisms also evolved during this time, from the first flowering plants to the flying pterosaurs, the ocean-dwelling ichthyosaurs and plesiosaurs, as well as the first mammals. In this section, you will discover many types of dinosaur and other ancient creatures, such as giant fish, sea-dwelling lizards, massive molluscs, and dinosaur-eating mammals, that lived during this era.

Often known as the Age of Dinosaurs, the Mesozoic Era is divided into three periods:
- Triassic (252–201 MYA) • Jurassic (201–143 MYA)
- Cretaceous (143–66 MYA)

Tyrannosaurus
TIE-ran-oh-SORE-us

Tyrannosaurus rex (or T. rex) is the most popular dinosaur of all. It lived at the very end of the Mesozoic Era, between 68 and 66 million years ago. More than 50 skeletons have been discovered in the USA and Canada, some of which are nearly complete. At 13 m (43 ft) long, T. rex was among the most fearsome predators ever to have walked on Earth.

Cretaceous Period · Land

T. rex's long tail helped to balance its large and heavy head.

Its skull was more than 1.5 m (5 ft) long.

Its teeth could crush through bone.

Triassic Period — Land

Herrerasaurus

heh-RARE-ra-SORE-uss

One of the first dinosaurs to appear, Herrerasaurus lived about 231 million years ago. Its fossils include skeletons and well-preserved skulls collected from the "Valley of the Moon" at the Ischigualasto Provincial Park, Argentina. Only a handful of the earliest dinosaurs have been found, with Herrerasaurus being one of the most complete and well studied.

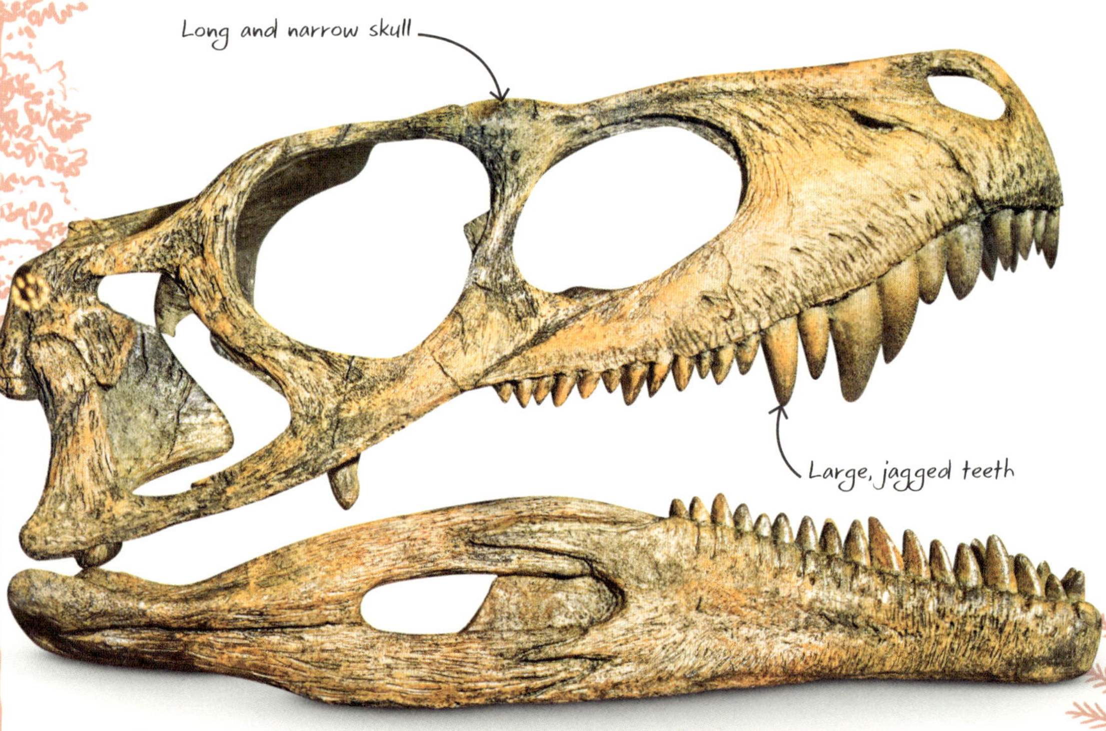

Long and narrow skull

Large, jagged teeth

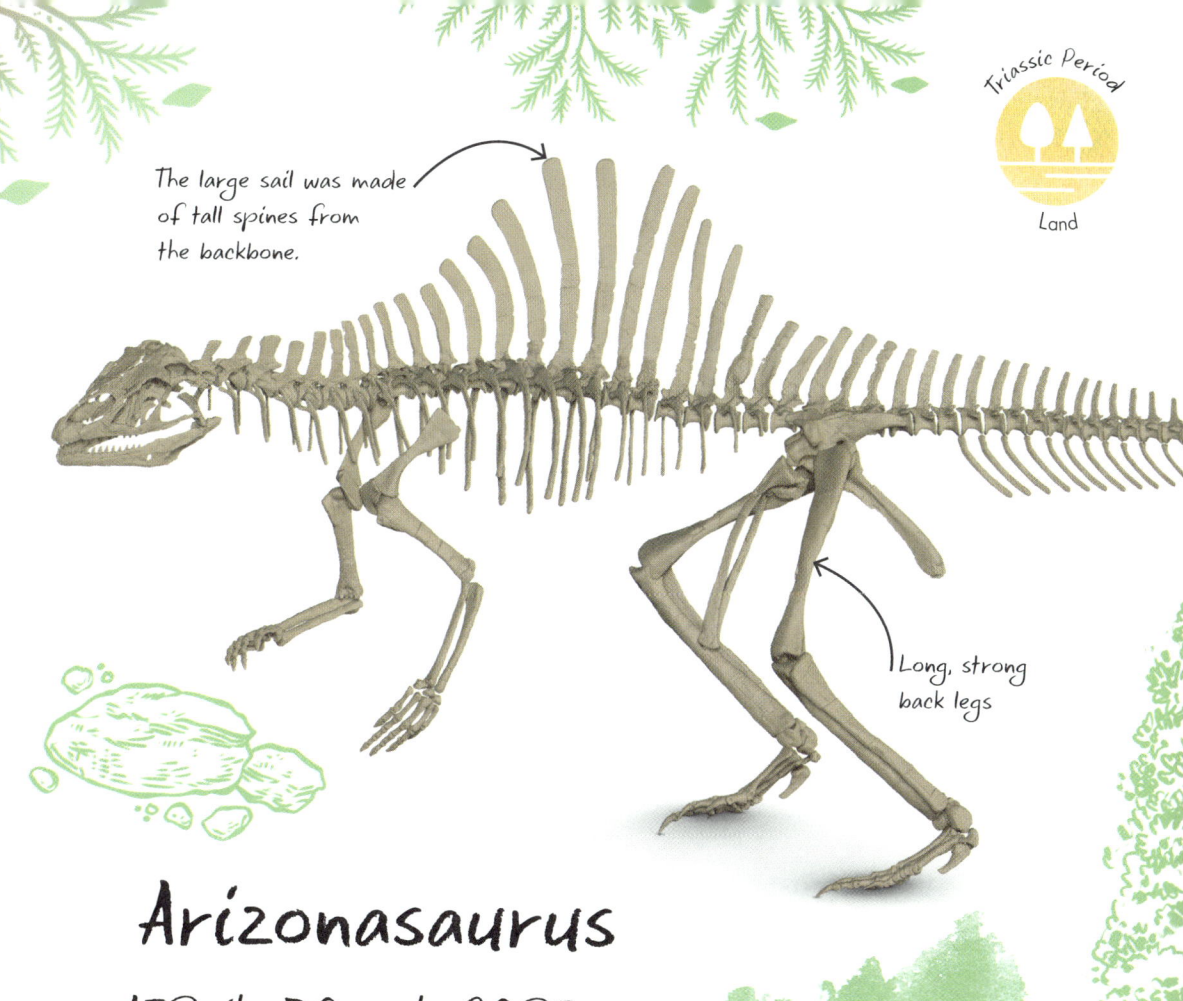

The large sail was made of tall spines from the backbone.

Long, strong back legs

Triassic Period

Land

Arizonasaurus

AIR-ih-ZO-nah-SORE-us

It might look similar to a Spinosaurus, but Arizonasaurus was not a dinosaur. It was actually a very distant relative of the crocodilians. Discovered in Arizona, USA, it was first described in 1947. For a long time, it was only identified from fossils of its teeth and a single jawbone. But, when an Arizonasaurus skeleton was found in 2002, more details about it were revealed.

Notes

- Arizonasaurus lived about 243 million years ago.
- It reached around 3 m (10 ft) in length.
- Crocodilians is a group of large reptiles, including crocodiles and alligators.

Triassic Period

Water

Land

Tanystropheus

tan-EE-stro-FEE-us

Tanystropheus was an unusual reptile with a neck longer than its body and tail combined. Since its discovery in 1852, it was thought to live either in water or on land. However, more recent evidence suggests it spent most of its time in water but also lived on land. Many of its fossils, including complete skeletons, come from Monte San Giorgio, which lies near the border of Switzerland and Italy. These fossils are around 240 million years old.

Tiny, rectangular head

Stiff neck made up of 13 long, narrow bones

One species of Tanystropheus was named *Tanystropheus hydroides* after a monster called Hydra in Greek mythology.

Upper arm bone

Notes

- Lisowicia was named after the village Lisowice in Poland, where its first fossils were found.
- This large land animal was more than 4.5 m (15 ft) long.

Triassic Period — Land

Lisowicia
li-so-WI-see-ah

In 2018, paleontologists discovered this enormous plant-eating ancestor of mammals that lived during the Late Triassic. Lisowicia was an exciting find as most known mammals and their relatives from this time were very small. Like modern mammals, Lisowicia had an erect, upright posture.

Jurassic Period–Today — Land

Ginkgo
GIN-koh

Appearing at least 200 million years ago, ginkgos are ancient trees that still exist today. They are easily identified by their fan-shaped leaves at the end of long, thin stems. Several species of ginkgo grew and spread widely during the Jurassic to Early Cretaceous Periods. Many fossils have been found on every continent, including Antarctica.

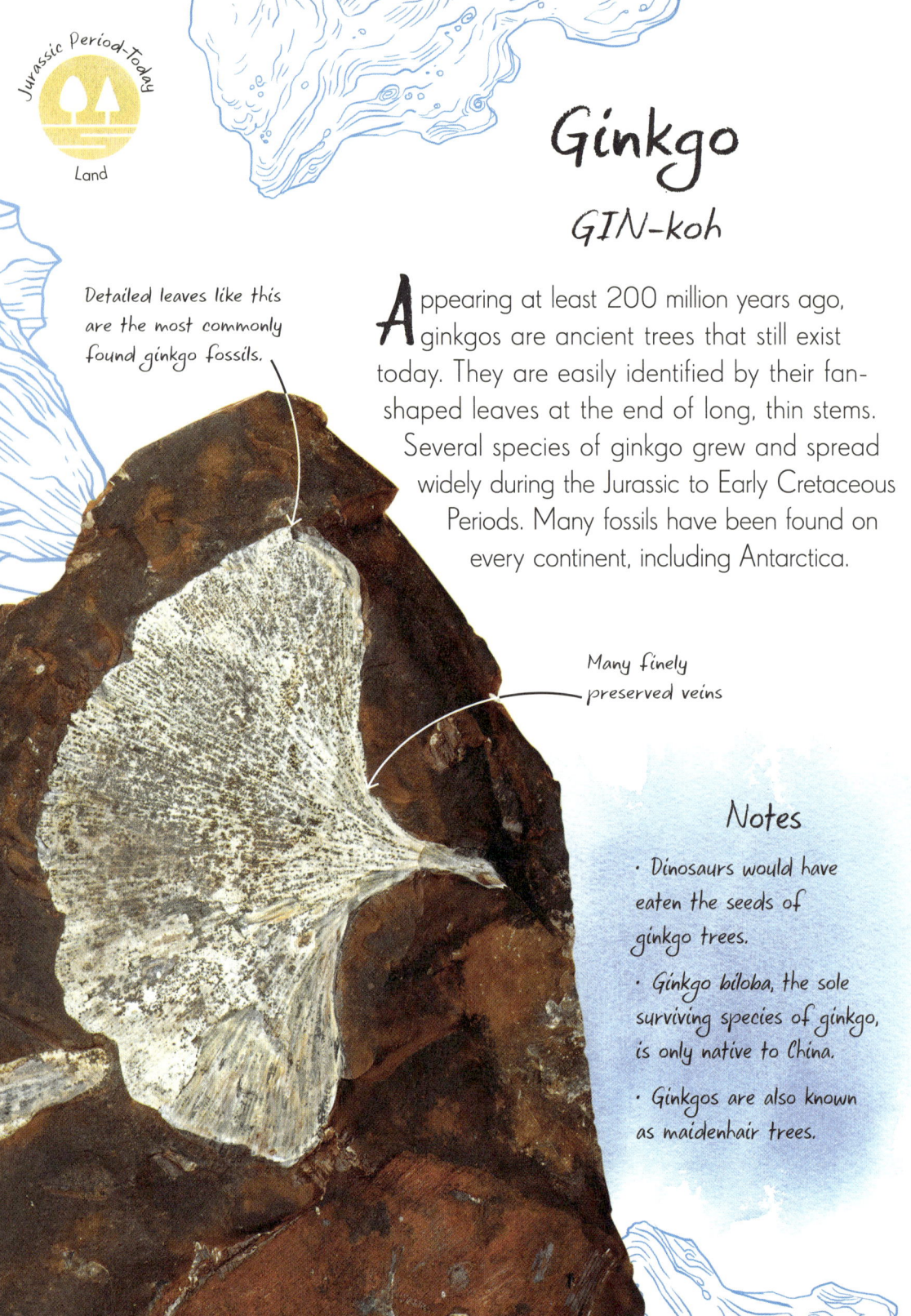

Detailed leaves like this are the most commonly found ginkgo fossils.

Many finely preserved veins

Notes

- Dinosaurs would have eaten the seeds of ginkgo trees.
- Ginkgo biloba, the sole surviving species of ginkgo, is only native to China.
- Ginkgos are also known as maidenhair trees.

Jurassic Period

Water

Its feathery arms were used to trap food.

The stems are commonly found as fossils.

Seirocrinus

sai-roh-KRY-nuss

Some Jurassic animals, such as Seirocrinus, are often mistaken for underwater plants due to their long stems and flower-like heads. However, they were actually crinoids. Some fossils unearthed in southern Germany show enormous Seirocrinus groups or colonies. The largest-known crinoid colony was about 20 m (66 ft) long.

The animal's feathery arms moved with the waves, while it was firmly held in place by a root-like structure.

Jurassic Period — Water

Ichthyosaurus

ICK-thee-oh-SORE-us

Ichthyosaurus gives its name to the group of ancient marine reptiles called ichthyosaurs. This shark-like reptile swam in the oceans around 200–185 million years ago. Many of its first fossils were uncovered by early fossil hunters, including paleontologist Mary Anning, who found many of the first ichthyosaurs.

Notes

- The largest species, Ichthyosaurus somersetensis, grew to 3.3 m (11 ft).
- One of the species, Ichthyosaurus anningae, was identified and named by Dr Dean Lomax and Professor Judy Massare.

Its big eyes helped it to hunt in dark waters.

Long jaw with cone-shaped teeth

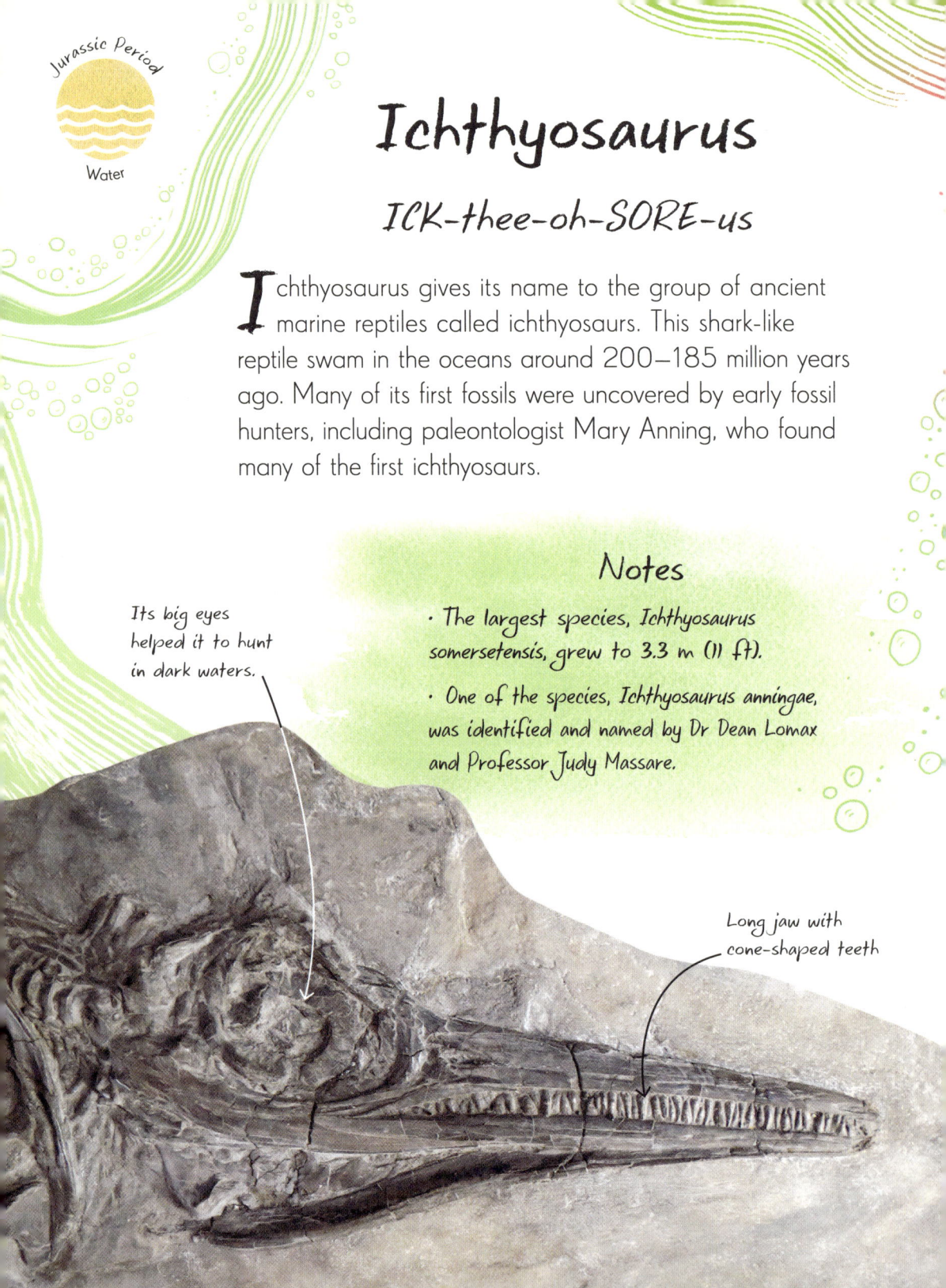

These grooves show where large muscles would have attached.

Triassic Period
Water

Ichthyotitan
ICK-thee-oh-TY-tan

Named in 2024, Ichthyotitan was a gigantic ichthyosaur that lived 202 million years ago. With a body length of about 25 m (82 ft), it was probably the largest marine reptile ever to have lived. Ichthyotitan is known from two enormous bones of the lower jaw. It went extinct at the very end of the Triassic.

Part of its lower jaw

Ichthyotitan was about the length of an average blue whale.

Record breakers

Fossils provide information about prehistoric life that helps to compare them with living animals. New discoveries can change what we know about ancient life. For instance, species that were once thought to be the largest may be replaced by more complete recent finds.

Longest claws

Therizinosaurus, a giraffe-sized theropod, is known to have the longest claws of any animal so far. The sickle-like claws were about 50 cm (20 in) long.

Therizinosaurus had three large claws on its two front limbs.

Largest dinosaur

The mighty Argentinosaurus is believed to be the largest dinosaur. It weighed as much as 12 African elephants and was about 35 m (115 ft) long. Its fossils have only been found in Argentina, hence the name.

Most complete giant sea reptile

This record belongs to the skeleton of Shonisaurus. Around 21 m (69 ft) long, the fossil was found in Canada. The giant lived during the Late Triassic and was the first enormous animal to appear.

A complete Keichousaurus fossil

One of the first mother fossils

Keichousaurus was a small marine reptile from the Middle Triassic. In 2004, two specimens were found with four and six embryos inside them. These were one of the first pregnant marine reptiles found in China.

First dino with colour

In 2010, the world's first-ever dinosaur with preserved colour was announced. Sinosauropteryx was one of the smallest dinosaurs. It had a covering of early feathers, also called dino fuzz. This tiny dinosaur was orange-red and white, with a striped tail.

Jurassic Period — Water

Leedsichthys used its round, stubby teeth to crush up food, like a nutcracker.

Leedsichthys

LEEDS-ick-thiss

Longer than a T. rex and one of the largest fish of all time, Leedsichthys had a body length of up to 16 m (52 ft). It was a ray-finned fish, a group of bony fish with fan-like fins. Leedsichthys is mostly known from fossil fragments and incomplete skeletons, including a massive 3-m (10-ft) tall tail fin.

Moving its gigantic tail fin from side to side, it had a top swimming speed of about 30 kph (19 mph).

Cretapsara

cret-ap-SA-rah

Cretaceous Period — Water — Land

Cretapsara was a type of crab that lived around 100–99 million years ago. The first fossil was found in 2021 inside amber. This was an incredible discovery as amber is mostly famous for preserving insects, and crabs are very rare. The fossil includes a complete crab with large eyes, delicate mouthparts, and gills.

Notes

- Cretapsara was the first crab discovered in Mesozoic amber.
- The amber fossil was collected from Myanmar, Southeast Asia.

The crab seemed to have been preserved in a freshwater environment.

Cretaceous Period

Water

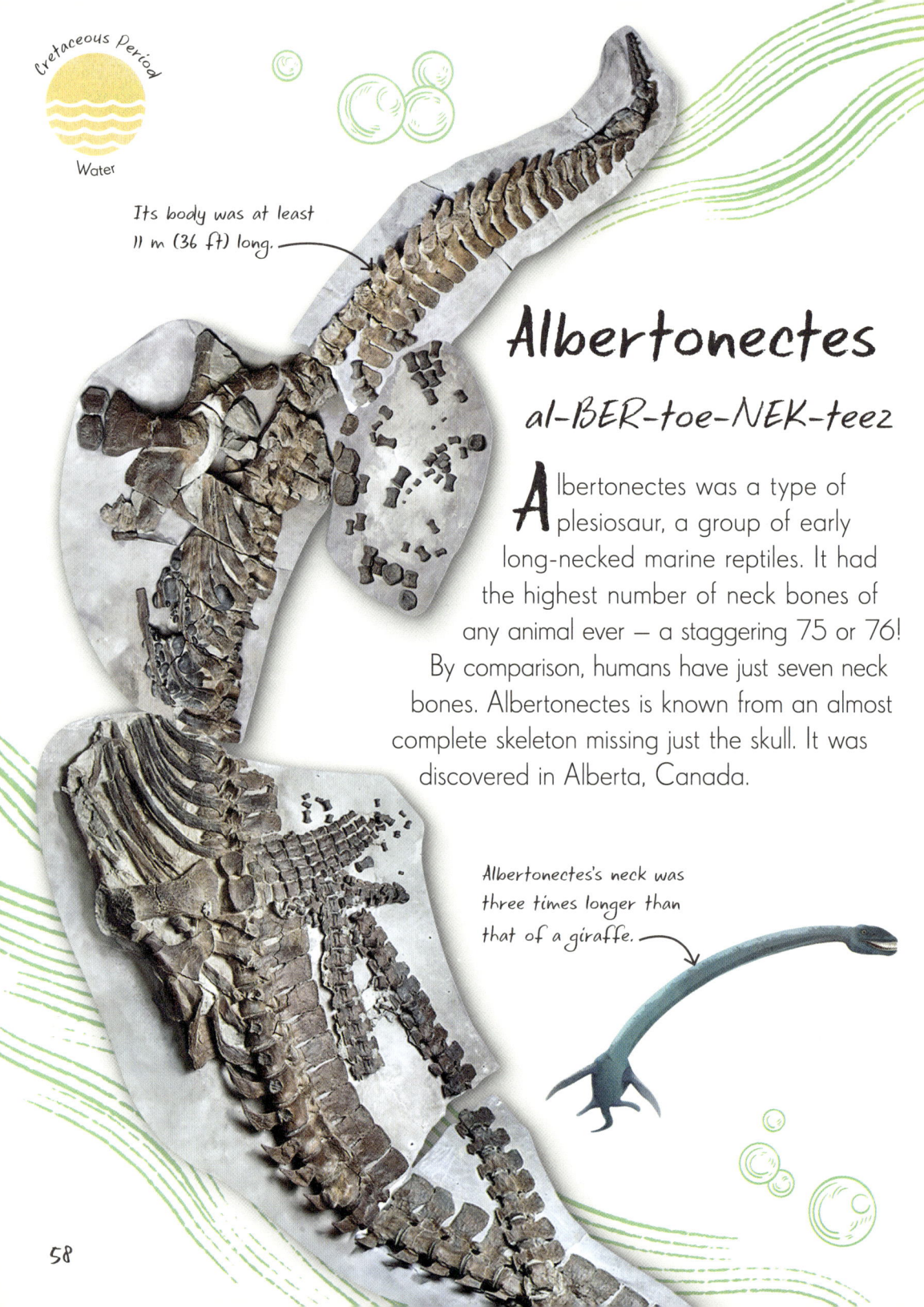

Its body was at least 11 m (36 ft) long.

Albertonectes

al-BER-toe-NEK-teez

Albertonectes was a type of plesiosaur, a group of early long-necked marine reptiles. It had the highest number of neck bones of any animal ever — a staggering 75 or 76! By comparison, humans have just seven neck bones. Albertonectes is known from an almost complete skeleton missing just the skull. It was discovered in Alberta, Canada.

Albertonectes's neck was three times longer than that of a giraffe.

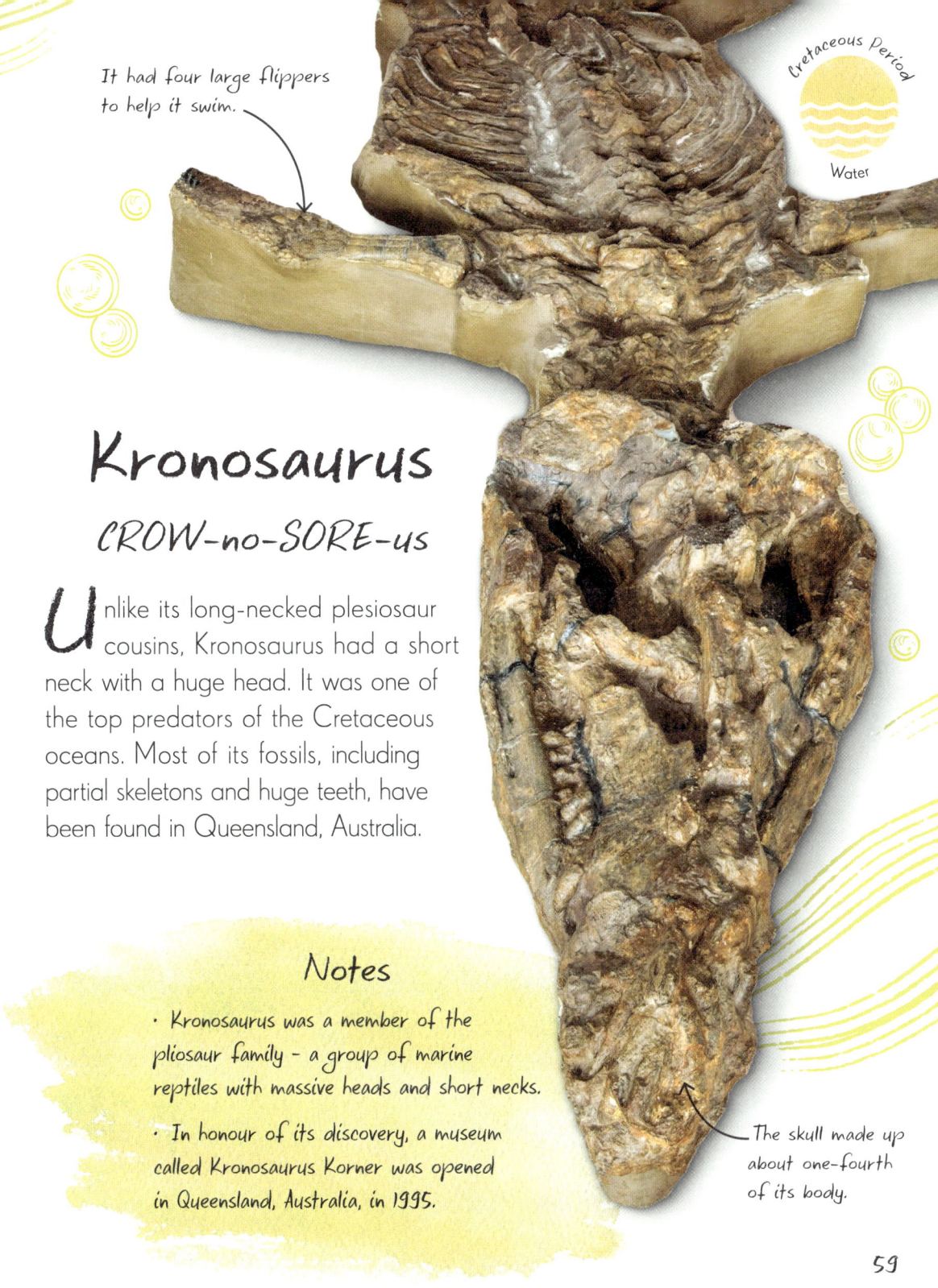

It had four large flippers to help it swim.

Cretaceous Period

Water

Kronosaurus

CROW-no-SORE-us

Unlike its long-necked plesiosaur cousins, Kronosaurus had a short neck with a huge head. It was one of the top predators of the Cretaceous oceans. Most of its fossils, including partial skeletons and huge teeth, have been found in Queensland, Australia.

Notes

- Kronosaurus was a member of the pliosaur family – a group of marine reptiles with massive heads and short necks.

- In honour of its discovery, a museum called Kronosaurus Korner was opened in Queensland, Australia, in 1995.

The skull made up about one-fourth of its body.

Jurassic Period — Water

Hildoceras

hill-DO-seh-russ

Hildoceras was a common ammonite. Ammonites are ancient marine animals that usually had spiral shells. There were multiple species of Hildoceras that lived during the Early Jurassic. Most of its fossils have been found at various sites across Europe and are especially abundant near the coastal town of Whitby in Yorkshire, England.

Multiple spiral grooves help scientists tell species apart

Notes

- Hildoceras was named after St. Hilda of Whitby, a patron saint of learning and culture.

- All ammonites lived their entire lives inside shells.

- Not all ammonites had perfect spiral shapes. Some had uncoiled, twisted, or straightened shells.

Jurassic Period

Water

Megateuthis

MEG-ah-too-thiss

Megateuthis is the largest of all known squid-like belemnites. Cousins of ammonites and modern molluscs, such as squid and cuttlefish, belemnite fossils are commonly known from a bullet-like structure called the guard or rostrum. This is the remnant of the animal's hard internal skeleton. Most belemnite fossils found are remains of the rostra, and often mistaken for dinosaur teeth.

Its rostrum was conical in shape.

The maximum body length of a Megateuthis might have been up to 3 m (10 ft).

The belemnite lived at the base of the rostrum.

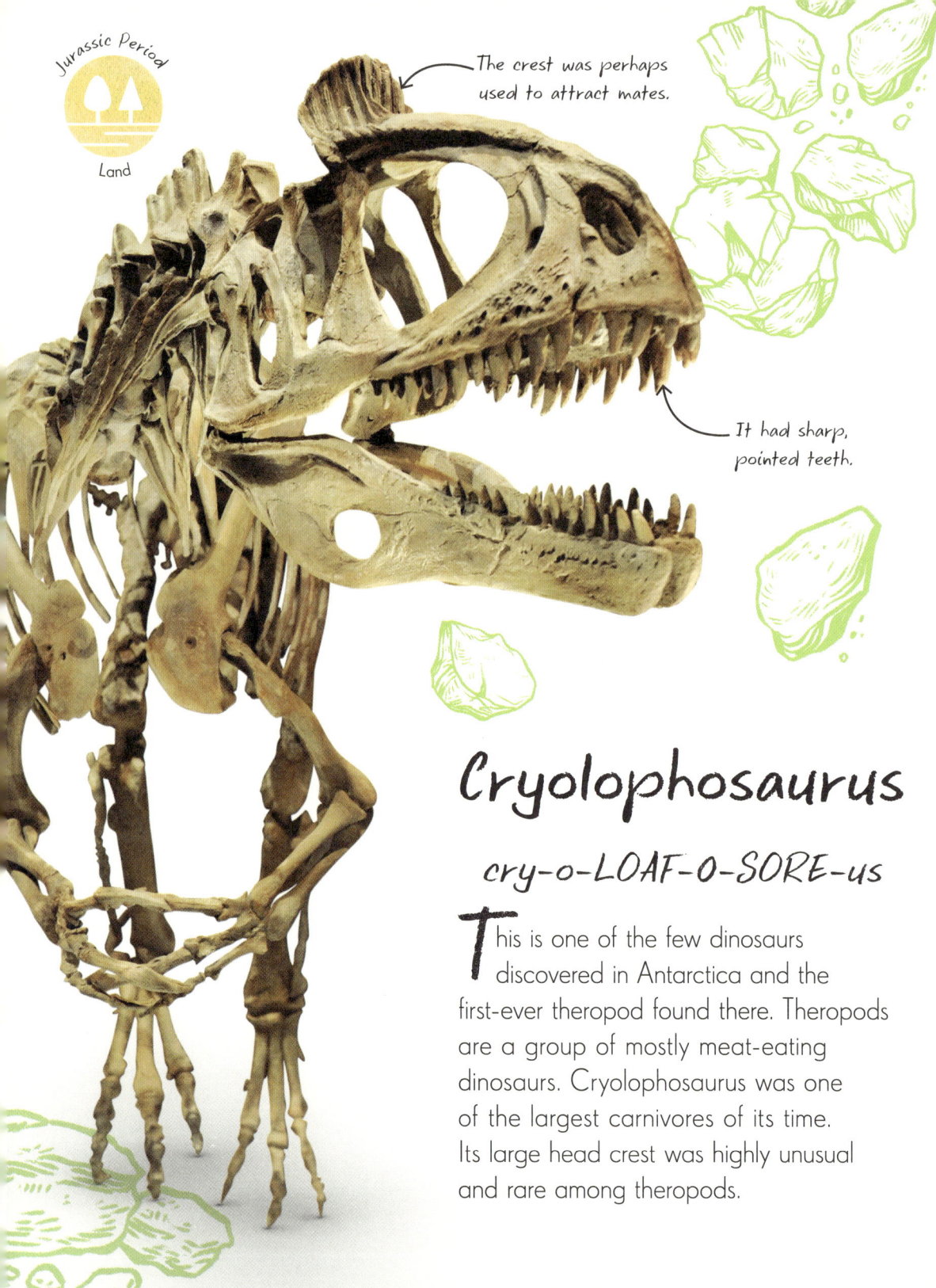

Jurassic Period — Land

The crest was perhaps used to attract mates.

It had sharp, pointed teeth.

Cryolophosaurus

cry-o-LOAF-o-SORE-us

This is one of the few dinosaurs discovered in Antarctica and the first-ever theropod found there. Theropods are a group of mostly meat-eating dinosaurs. Cryolophosaurus was one of the largest carnivores of its time. Its large head crest was highly unusual and rare among theropods.

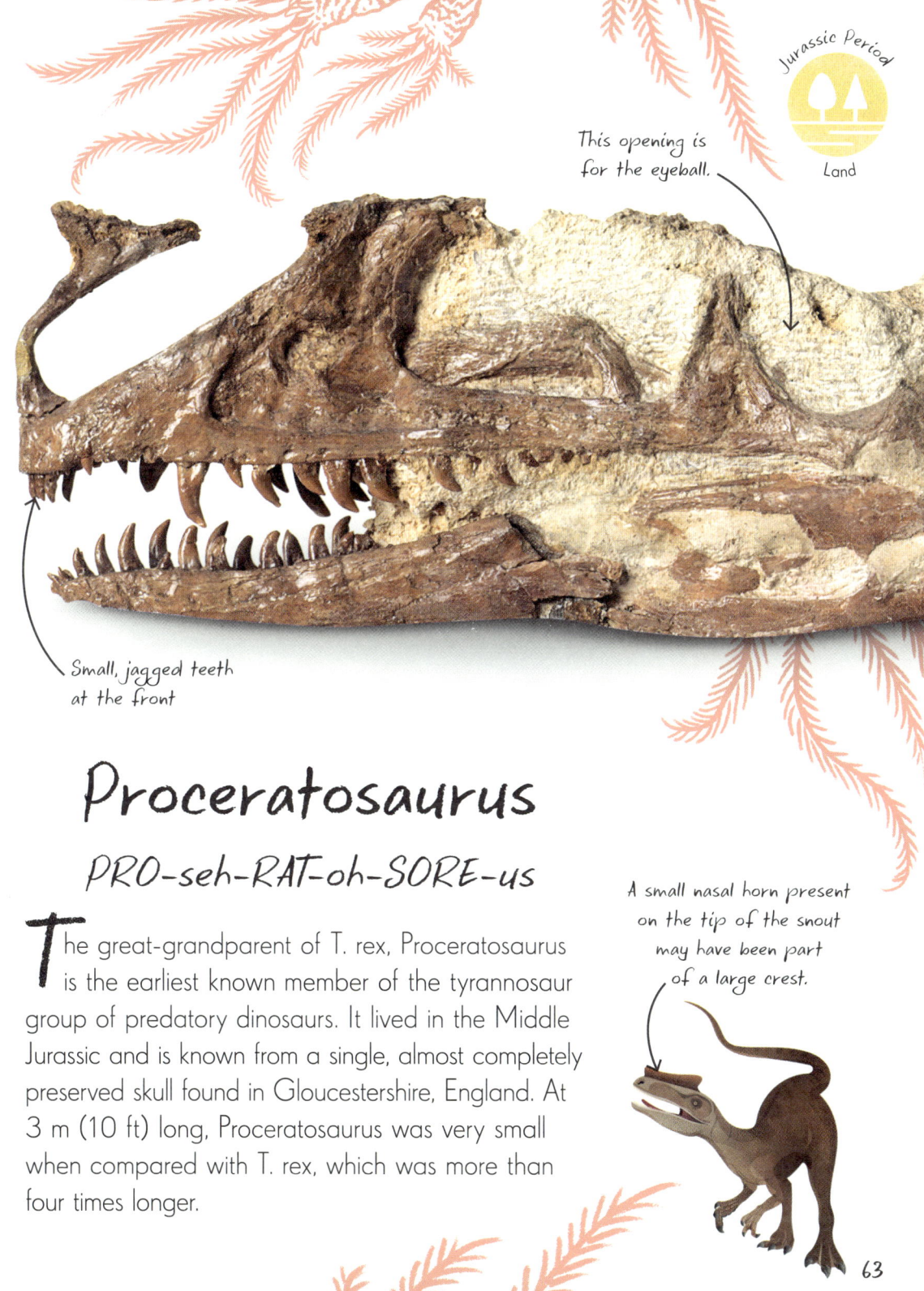

Jurassic Period
Land

This opening is for the eyeball.

Small, jagged teeth at the front

Proceratosaurus
PRO-seh-RAT-oh-SORE-us

The great-grandparent of T. rex, Proceratosaurus is the earliest known member of the tyrannosaur group of predatory dinosaurs. It lived in the Middle Jurassic and is known from a single, almost completely preserved skull found in Gloucestershire, England. At 3 m (10 ft) long, Proceratosaurus was very small when compared with T. rex, which was more than four times longer.

A small nasal horn present on the tip of the snout may have been part of a large crest.

Studying behaviour

There are rare instances where fossils help us learn about past behaviours. For example, some fossils may contain remains of an organism's last meal or signs of an attack, such as a tooth stuck in the bone of another animal. These fossils provide evidence of ancient animal behaviours, also known as paleoethology.

Dino duels

One of the most legendary fossils of all time was discovered in the Gobi Desert in Central Asia. A turkey-sized Velociraptor was found to be locked in a fight with a boar-sized Protoceratops. The fossil records the Protoceratops biting the arm of the Velociraptor, who in turn is slashing the Protoceratops with its sickle claw.

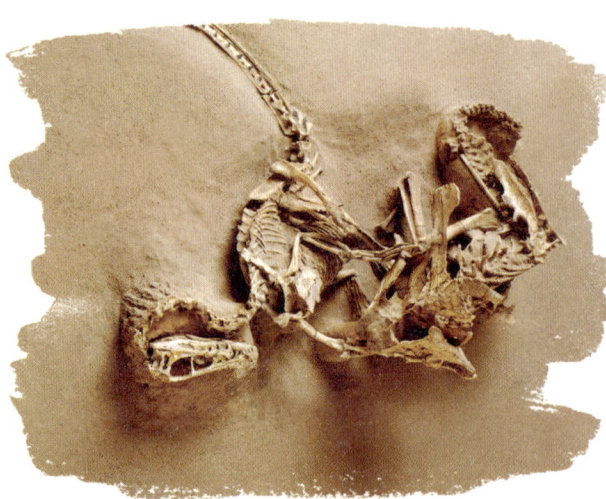

Eggs preserved on the legs

Cared for young

At a famous fossil site in China, six lobster-like creatures, called Kunmingella, were found with preserved eggs. As many as 180 tiny eggs were attached to their legs, which showed that they looked after their eggs about 520 million years ago.

Feeding

Around 150 million years ago, in what is today southern Germany, a pterosaur named Rhamphorhynchus snatched a small fish from the water. At the very moment, a much larger fish called Aspidorhynchus caught the pterosaur. Incredibly, five similar fossils have been found.

A fossil of an Aspidorhynchus grabbing a pterosaur

Travelled in herds

Many dinosaur footprints have been found at sites around the world. Some discoveries have revealed that dinosaurs, such as sauropods, travelled in large groups or families.

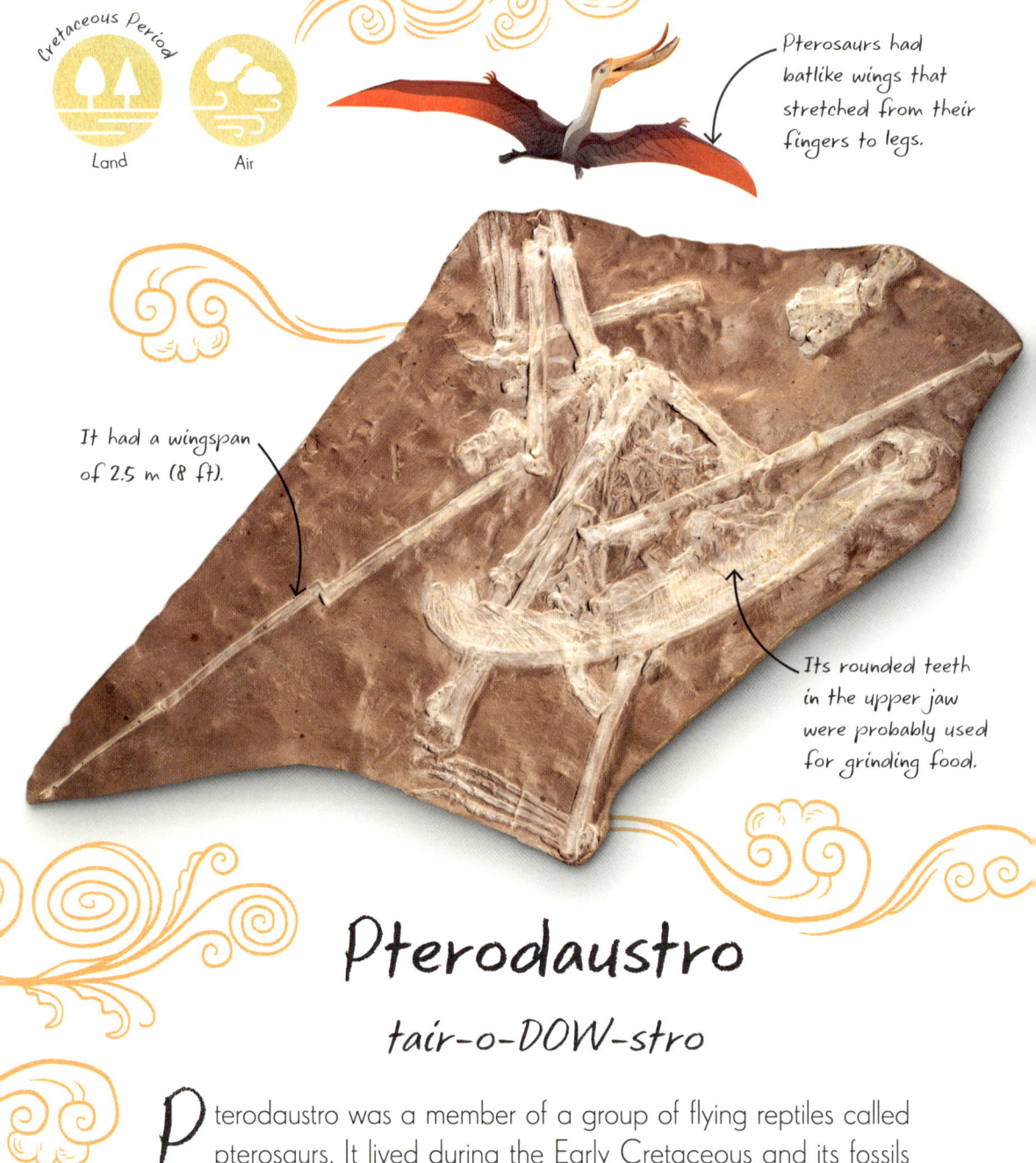

Cretaceous Period

Land

Air

Pterosaurs had batlike wings that stretched from their fingers to legs.

It had a wingspan of 2.5 m (8 ft).

Its rounded teeth in the upper jaw were probably used for grinding food.

Pterodaustro

tair-o-DOW-stro

Pterodaustro was a member of a group of flying reptiles called pterosaurs. It lived during the Early Cretaceous and its fossils have been found in Argentina. It had slender, upward-curving jaws with about 1,000 needlelike teeth. This is one of the most well-studied pterosaurs and hundreds of its fossils have been found.

Confuciusornis
con-FEW-shus-OR-niss

Cretaceous Period
Land

Air

About the size of a crow, this magnificent fossil bird was described in 1995. Confuciusornis had a toothless beak like modern birds. The fossil was preserved with long wing feathers and discovered at a famous fossil site in Liaoning Province, China. Several thousand Confuciusornis fossils have been identified so far.

It had a wingspan of about 70 cm (28 in).

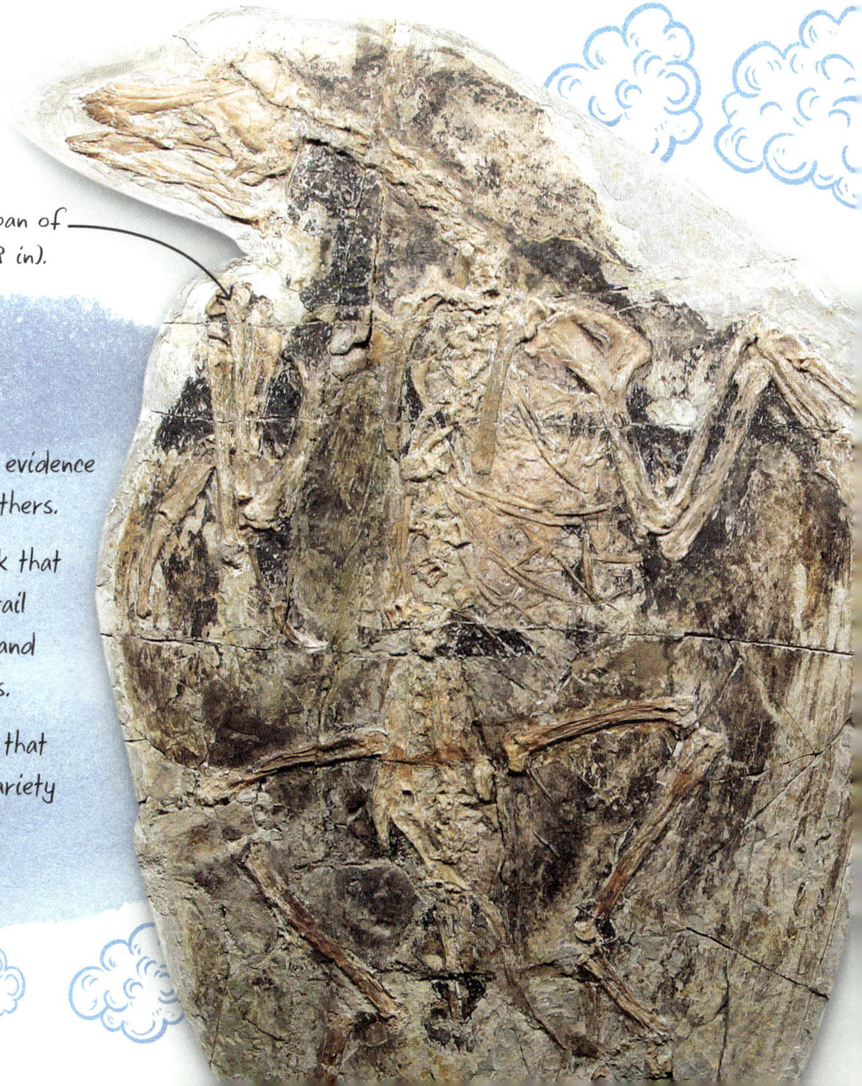

Notes

- Some fossils reveal evidence of scaly skin and feathers.

- Paleontologists think that specimens with long tail feathers were males and the rest were females.

- One fossil revealed that the feathers had a variety of patterns on them.

Jurassic Period — Land

Hesperornithoides

HESS-per-ORE-nee-THOY-deez

In 2001, a pigeon-sized dinosaur skeleton was discovered in Wyoming, USA. This one-of-a-kind fossil represented a new type of dinosaur. It was named Hesperornithoides in 2019 by a team that included Dr Dean Lomax. A cousin of Velociraptor, this birdlike dinosaur lived alongside many popular dinosaurs, such as Stegosaurus and Allosaurus.

Its sickle-shaped claw was probably used to grip prey.

Its head could fit in the palm of a human hand.

Notes

- Hesperornithoides is the smallest dinosaur found in Wyoming, USA.
- The skeleton was nicknamed "Lori" in honour of a volunteer who helped with the dig.

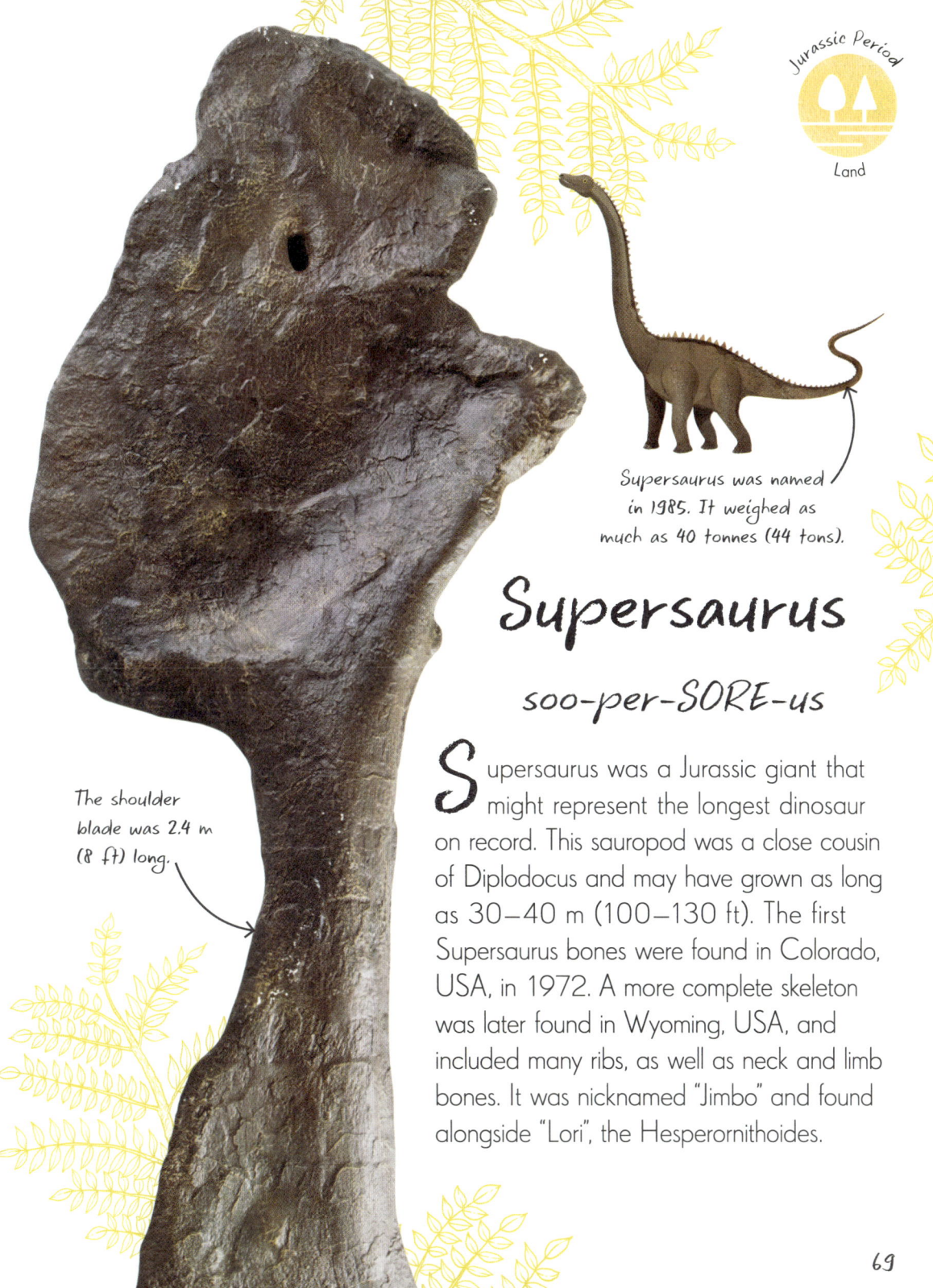

Jurassic Period

Land

Supersaurus was named in 1985. It weighed as much as 40 tonnes (44 tons).

Supersaurus

soo-per-SORE-us

Supersaurus was a Jurassic giant that might represent the longest dinosaur on record. This sauropod was a close cousin of Diplodocus and may have grown as long as 30–40 m (100–130 ft). The first Supersaurus bones were found in Colorado, USA, in 1972. A more complete skeleton was later found in Wyoming, USA, and included many ribs, as well as neck and limb bones. It was nicknamed "Jimbo" and found alongside "Lori", the Hesperornithoides.

The shoulder blade was 2.4 m (8 ft) long.

Cretaceous Period
Land

Short limbs

Its sharp teeth were used to snatch and tear apart prey.

Repenomamus

rep-EN-oh-mam-uss

When we think of mammals from the Mesozoic Era, we usually think of tiny, mouse-sized animals. This changed in 2000 with the discovery of Repenomamus, a badger-sized mammal from the Cretaceous Period in China. It was a giant among the mammals of its time and even dined on dinosaurs. One extraordinary fossil was found with baby dinosaurs inside its gut.

Baby Maiasaura used its tiny teeth to munch plants and leaves.

Its hind legs became stronger over time.

Cretaceous Period — Land

Maiasaura

MY-a-SORE-a

With its duck-like, flat mouth, Maiasaura is one of the most famous hadrosaurs (or duck-billed dinosaurs). It is best known from the many skeletons, as well as from the discovery of a Maiasaura nesting site in Montana, USA. The preserved eggs and babies in nests revealed that the adults lived in colonies and cared for their young.

Notes

- Maiasaura was named in 1979 and it means "good mother lizard".

- Nests typically contained 30 to 40 ostrich-sized eggs that were laid in a circle.

- Adults guarded their nests from predators.

Jurassic Period — Land

Miragaia

mih-RA-gai-ah

A cousin of the famous Stegosaurus, Miragaia is a type of armoured dinosaur called a stegosaur. It gets its name from the Portuguese village of Miragaia, where the fossils were found. With at least 17 neck bones, it has the longest neck of all known stegosaurs. Miragaia had two rows of tall plates along its back, and spikes at the end of its tail.

The plates on its back were used for defence against predators.

Bones of the skull and parts of the skeleton have been found

Zuul

ZOOL

Cretaceous Period — Land

With sharp spikes on its body and a large tail club, Zuul was an ankylosaur (another family of armoured dinosaurs). Only one almost complete Zuul fossil is known, which was discovered in northern Montana, USA, in 2014. This unique fossil preserves a huge bony shield of armour with skin and spikes.

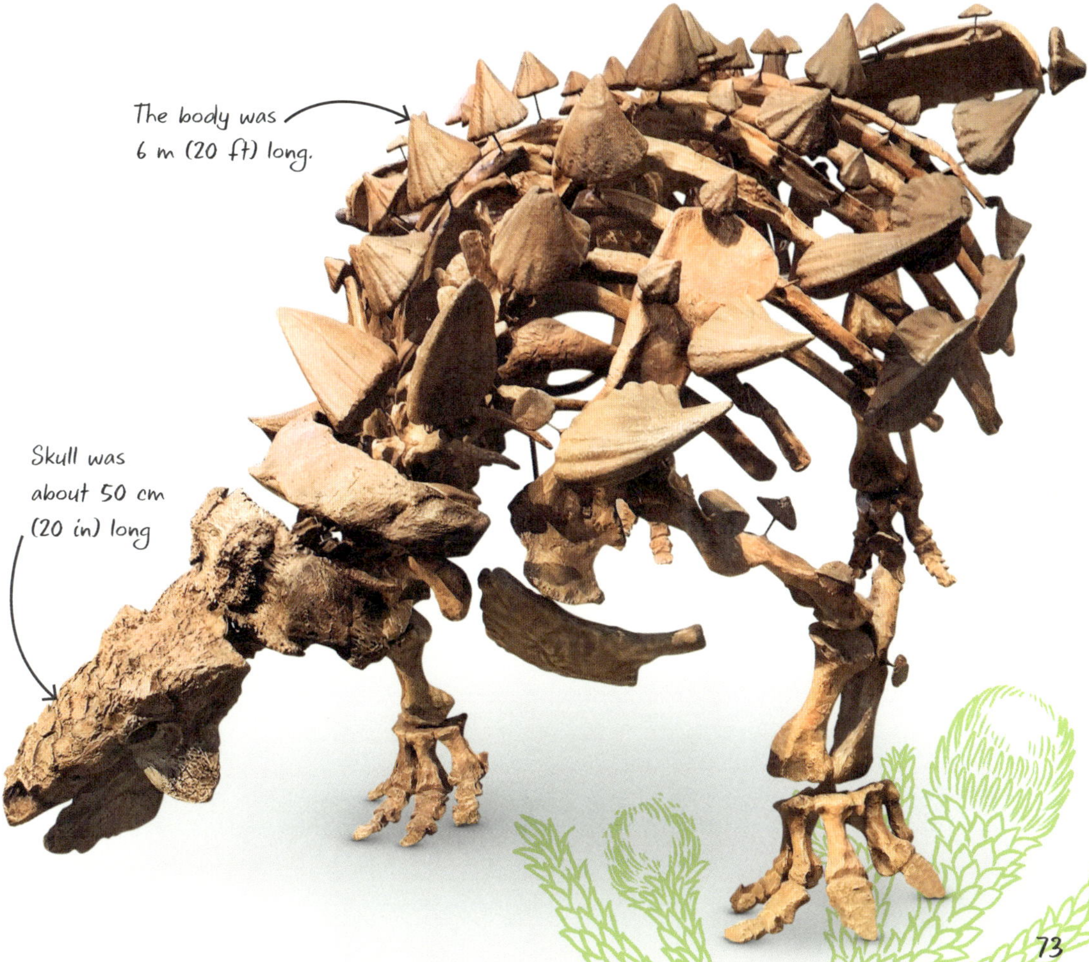

The body was 6 m (20 ft) long.

Skull was about 50 cm (20 in) long

Jurassic Period — Land, Air

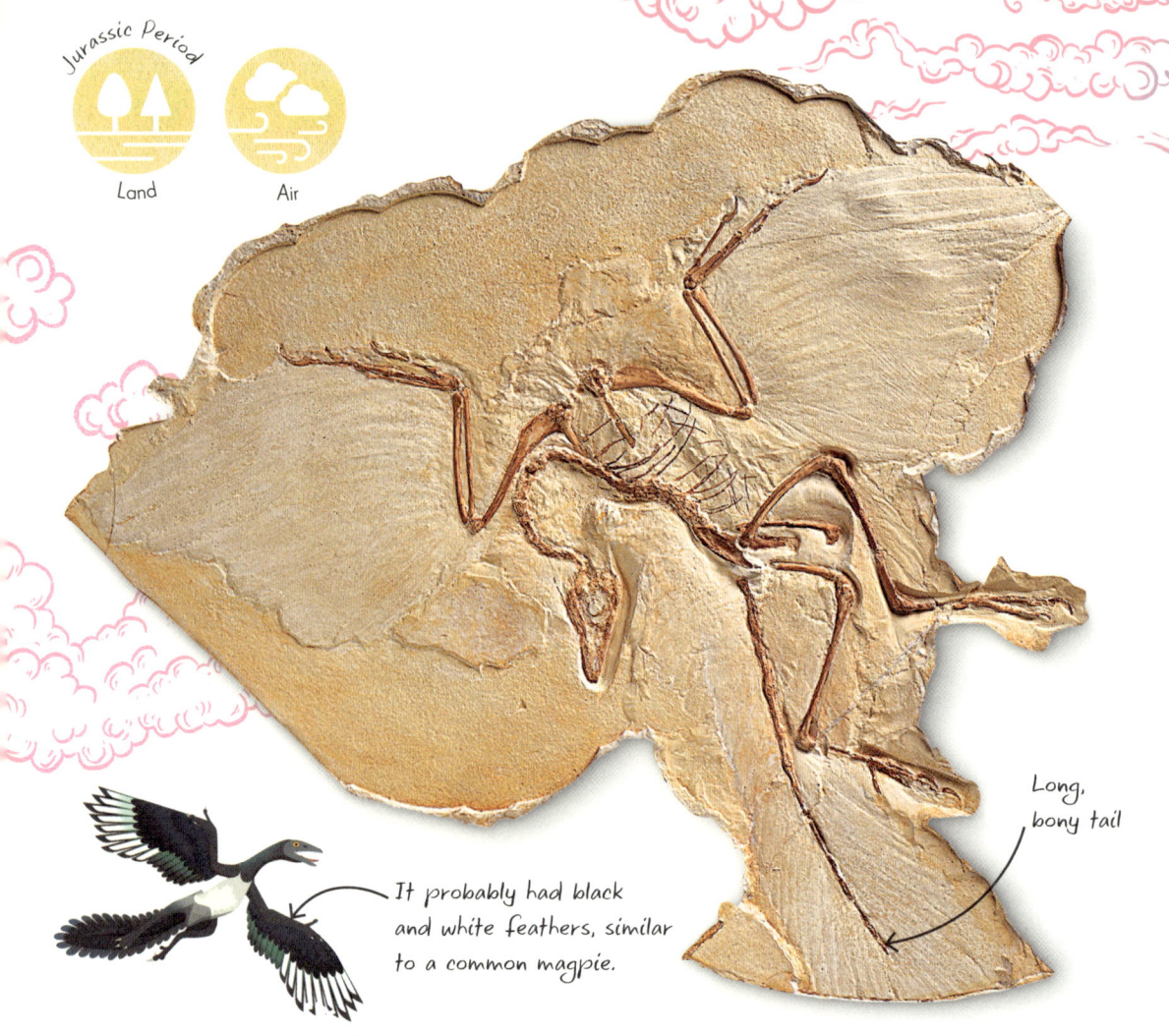

Long, bony tail

It probably had black and white feathers, similar to a common magpie.

Archaeopteryx

ar-kee-OP-ter-ix

Archaeopteryx had wings and a long, feathered tail like a bird and sharp teeth like its dinosaur cousins. It was the first fossil to provide a link between birds and dinosaurs. In 1861, Archaeopteryx's first nearly complete fossil was found by a farmer in southern Germany, who later sold it to buy a cow!

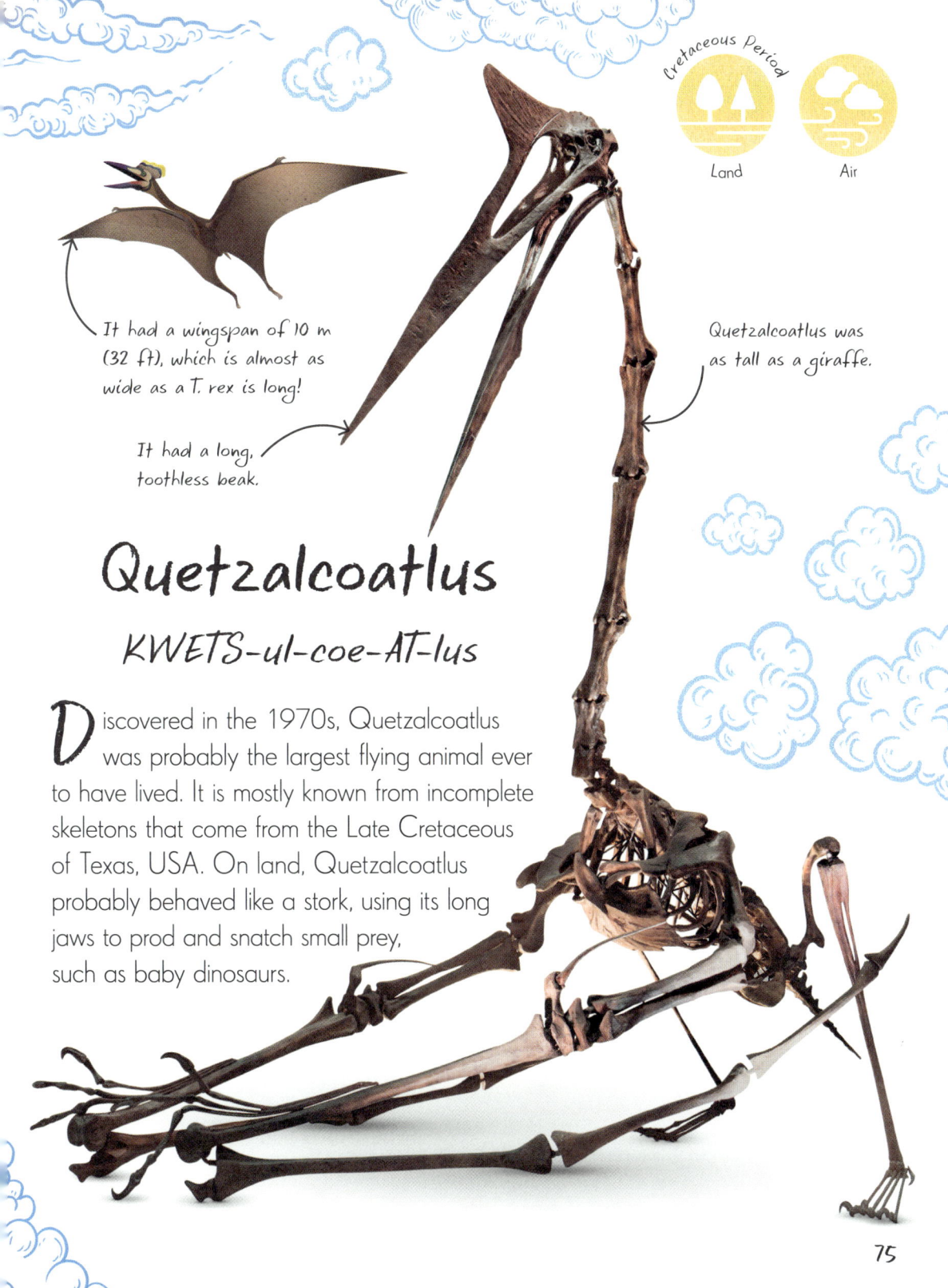

Land Air

Cretaceous Period

It had a wingspan of 10 m (32 ft), which is almost as wide as a T. rex is long!

It had a long, toothless beak.

Quetzalcoatlus was as tall as a giraffe.

Quetzalcoatlus

KWETS-ul-coe-AT-lus

Discovered in the 1970s, Quetzalcoatlus was probably the largest flying animal ever to have lived. It is mostly known from incomplete skeletons that come from the Late Cretaceous of Texas, USA. On land, Quetzalcoatlus probably behaved like a stork, using its long jaws to prod and snatch small prey, such as baby dinosaurs.

Cretaceous Period
Water

Xiphactinus
zye-FAC-tee-nus

Named in 1870, Xiphactinus is sometimes known as the bulldog-like fish due to its upturned jaw. This large fish reached sizes of up to 6 m (20 ft). Many well-preserved, complete skeletons have been discovered in Kansas, USA, which was once covered by a shallow sea during the Late Cretaceous.

A strong tail helped it to swim fast.

Large, fang-like teeth

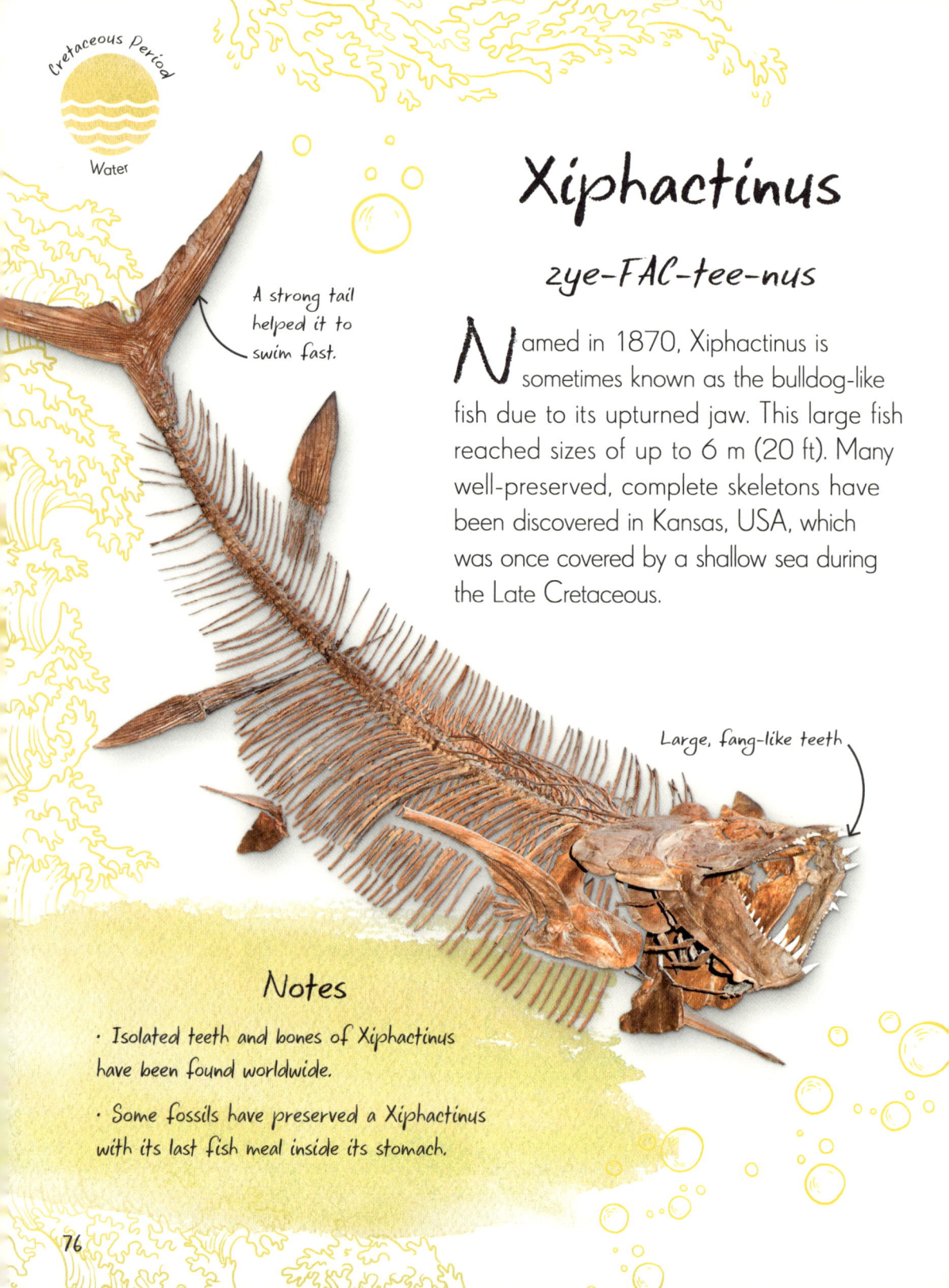

Notes

- Isolated teeth and bones of Xiphactinus have been found worldwide.
- Some fossils have preserved a Xiphactinus with its last fish meal inside its stomach.

Cretaceous Period

Water

Bone-crunching teeth

Tylosaurus

TIE-lo-SORE-us

Tylosaurus was a gigantic marine lizard that belonged to an extinct family of aquatic reptiles called mosasaurs. Numerous skeletons and isolated bones, mostly found in the USA, suggest that this reptile grew to a length of 12–15 m (40–50 ft). Fossilized bite marks show that Tylosaurus dined on giant sea turtles, big fish, and other mosasaurs.

One Tylosaurus fossil shows that it had diamond-shaped scales, similar to modern snakes.

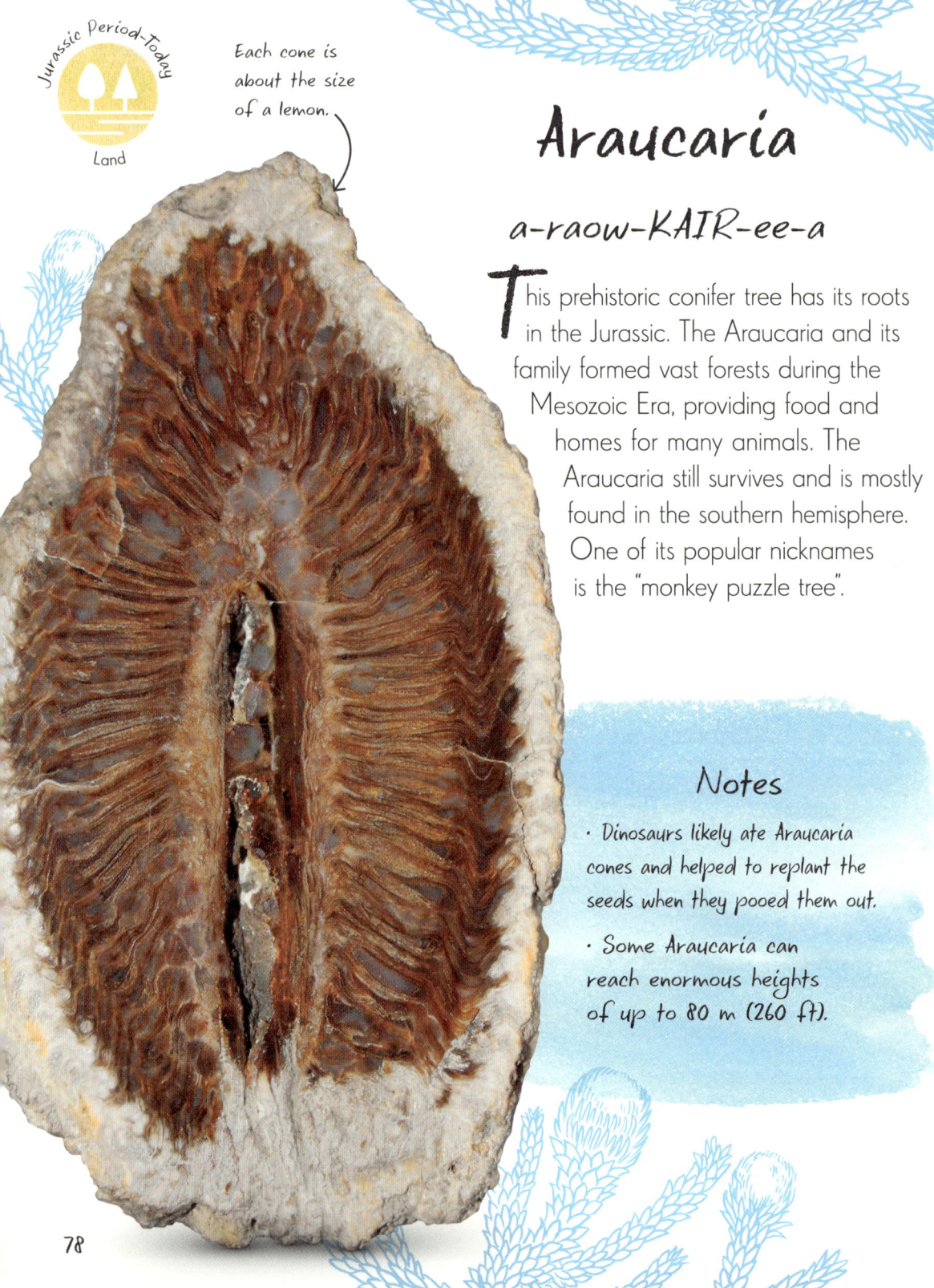

Jurassic Period-Today — Land

Each cone is about the size of a lemon.

Araucaria

a-raow-KAIR-ee-a

This prehistoric conifer tree has its roots in the Jurassic. The Araucaria and its family formed vast forests during the Mesozoic Era, providing food and homes for many animals. The Araucaria still survives and is mostly found in the southern hemisphere. One of its popular nicknames is the "monkey puzzle tree".

Notes

- Dinosaurs likely ate Araucaria cones and helped to replant the seeds when they pooed them out.

- Some Araucaria can reach enormous heights of up to 80 m (260 ft).

Finely preserved veins can be seen in this fossil leaf.

Oval-shaped leaf

Magnolia
mag-NOH-lee-a

Magnolia is an ancient flowering plant. Members of this family appeared during the Cretaceous. Beetles carried pollen from these flowers, which helped make seeds so new plants could grow. Many Magnolia fossils, including wood, flowers, and leaves, have been found.

Cretaceous Period — Land

Lokiceratops

low-key-SEH-ra-tops

Named in 2024, Lokiceratops is one of the most recently discovered horned dinosaurs, or ceratopsians. It lived 78 million years ago, about 10 million years before its larger cousin Triceratops. So far, only a single specimen has been found, which includes a skull and part of a skeleton.

Two big, curved horns on its head

The frill may have been used to ward off predators.

At almost 7 m (23 ft) long, Lokiceratops was about twice the length of an average rhinoceros.

Parasaurolophus
PA-ra-SORE-oh-LOAF-us

Cretaceous Period
Land

Measuring about 10 m (33 ft) long, Parasaurolophus was one of the largest hadrosaurs. It was one of the few dinosaurs to have a long, bony crest on its head. In 2009, a high school student in Utah, USA, found the first nearly complete skeleton of a baby Parasaurolophus. This extremely rare fossil revealed that the crest was much smaller and more bump-like in young dinosaurs.

The long, hollow head crest may have been used to produce trumpet-like sounds.

Its multiple rows of teeth helped to chew plants.

Water · Land

Deinosuchus

DIE-no-SOO-kuss

Deadly Deinosuchus was a giant crocodilian with a bone-crunching bite. Measuring 10 m (33 ft) long, it was one of the largest crocodilians ever to have existed. Deinosuchus was a close relative of modern-day alligators, but was much larger. Hundreds of Deinosuchus fossils have been uncovered in the USA and Mexico. These include skulls, partial skeletons, and many large teeth.

Notes

- Deinosuchus lived between 75 and 82 million years ago.
- Deinosuchus fed on dinosaurs, fish, turtles, and anything else it could catch.
- It was almost twice the length of a saltwater crocodile, the largest living crocodilian.

Its bite force was about five times stronger than a saltwater crocodile.

Used its short and powerful limbs to drag itself onto riverbanks

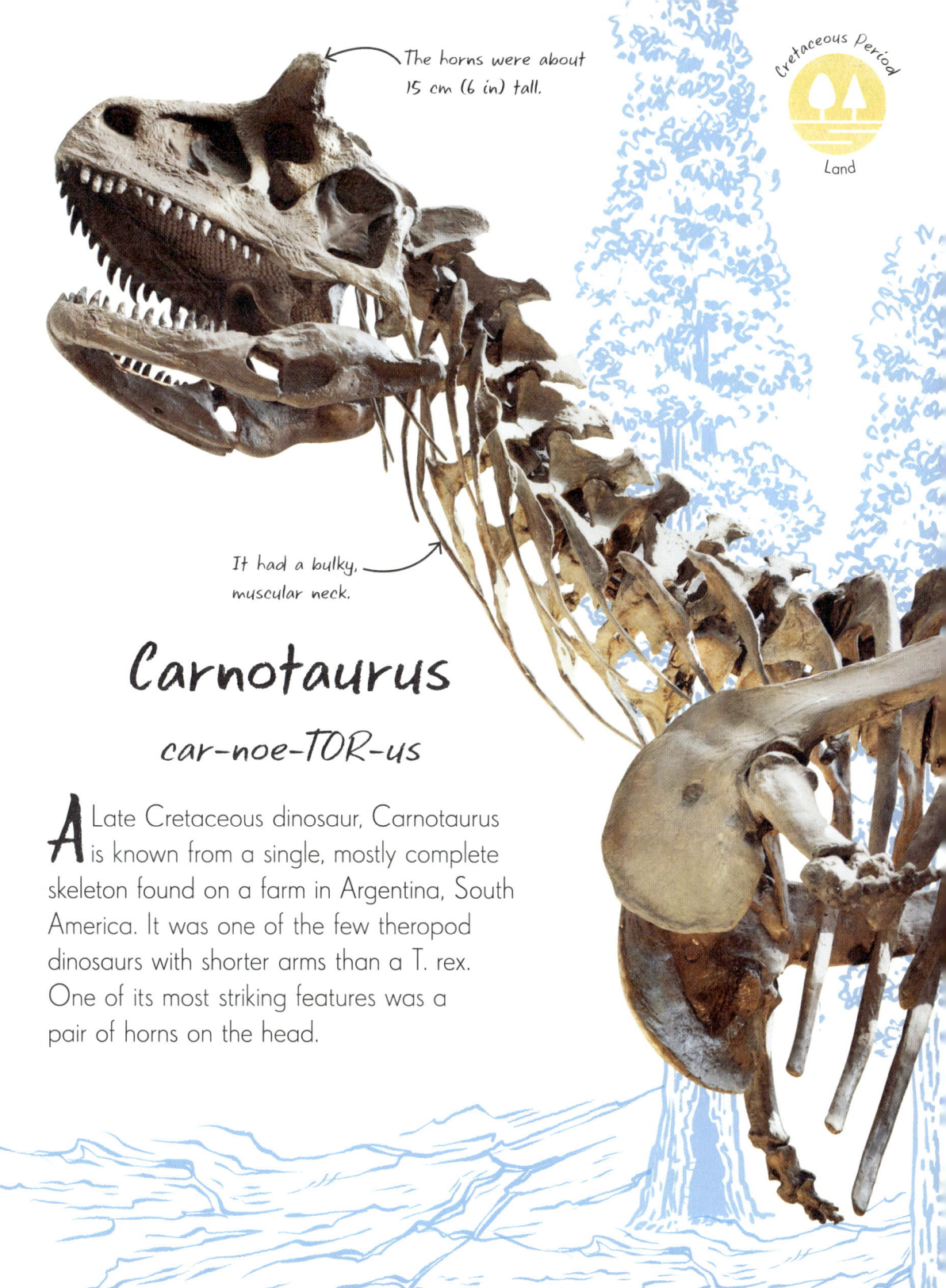

The horns were about 15 cm (6 in) tall.

Cretaceous Period
Land

It had a bulky, muscular neck.

Carnotaurus
car-noe-TOR-us

A Late Cretaceous dinosaur, Carnotaurus is known from a single, mostly complete skeleton found on a farm in Argentina, South America. It was one of the few theropod dinosaurs with shorter arms than a T. rex. One of its most striking features was a pair of horns on the head.

Cretaceous Period
Land

Its big eyes were ideal for spotting prey, even at night.

Velociraptor had about 60 sharp teeth.

Velociraptor

vel-OSS-ee-RAP-tor

A swift and speedy hunter, Velociraptor used its wings to run quickly, not fly. Its fossils were first unearthed in 1923 in the Gobi Desert, Central Asia. More than 10 skeletons have been found, along with many isolated bones, skulls, and teeth. Often thought to have been a human-sized predator, Velociraptor was in fact the size of a turkey but with a long tail.

The sickle-shaped claw on its second toe would have been used to pin down and stab prey.

Spinosaurus

SPINE-oh-SORE-us

The largest theropod discovered to date, Spinosaurus was among the strangest meat-eating dinosaurs. It had a huge sail on its back, a crocodile-like snout, and a fin-like tail. The first Spinosaurus fossils were found in 1912 in Egypt, but were unfortunately destroyed during World War II. Recent fossils have been found in Morocco, Africa, which have provided more details about this dinosaur.

Notes

- Spinosaurus would have spent part of its time in the water and dined on large fish.
- Its huge sail may have helped it to warm up or cool down.

The nostrils located high on its snout helped it breathe underwater.

Sharp, conical teeth

Cretaceous Period
Land

Triceratops

try-SERRA-tops

Measuring about 9 m (30 ft) in length, Triceratops is probably the largest-known ceratopsian. It also appears to have had the longest skull of any land animal on record — about 2.5 m (8 ft). Triceratops lived at the very end of the Cretaceous, along with other famous dinosaurs, such as T. rex and Ankylosaurus.

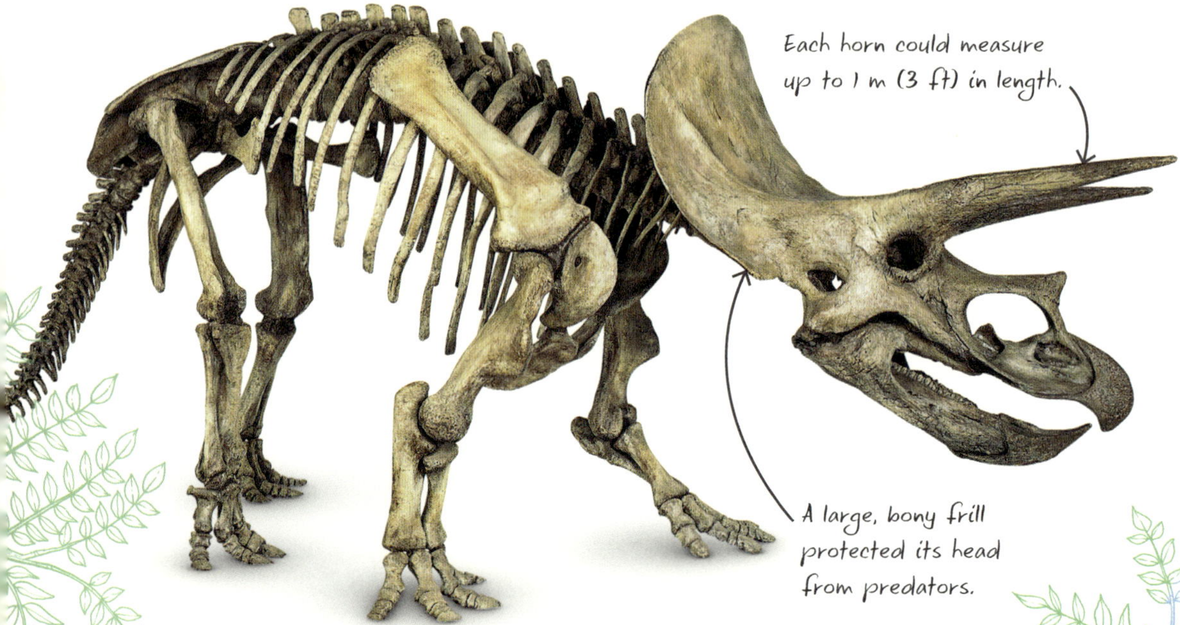

Each horn could measure up to 1 m (3 ft) in length.

A large, bony frill protected its head from predators.

Bony spikes on its snout and around the skull may have been used to show off.

Cretaceous Period
Land

Its skull was 60 cm (24 in) long.

Pachycephalosaurus

PACK-ee-SEF-ah-low-SORE-us

Known for its extremely thick, domed skull, Pachycephalosaurus is the largest member of the dinosaur family called pachycephalosaurs. All its known fossils have been found in western North America, dating back to the very end of the Cretaceous. These fossils are represented by isolated skulls.

Pachycephalosaurus probably used its skull to head-butt or side-ram others.

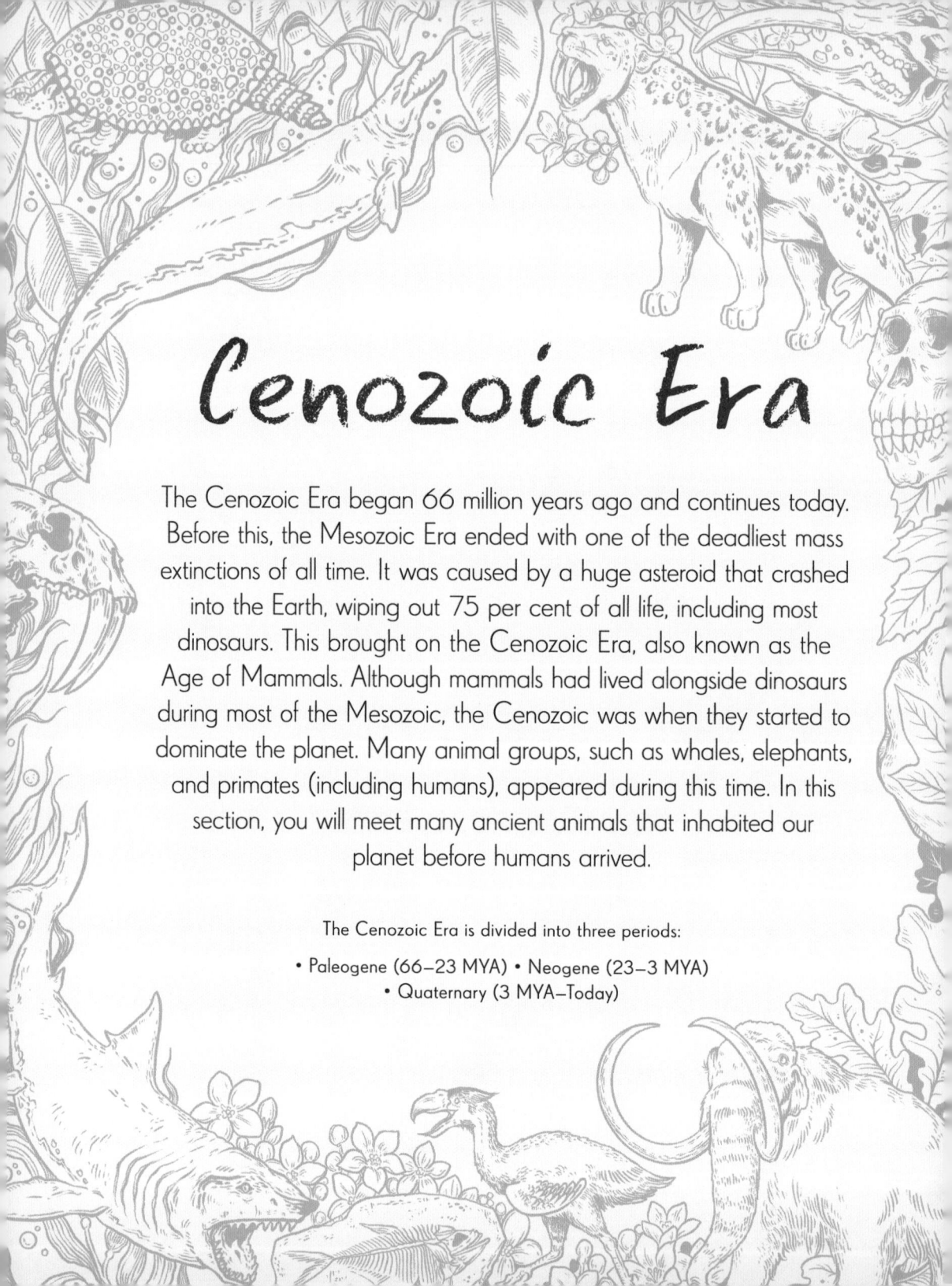

Cenozoic Era

The Cenozoic Era began 66 million years ago and continues today. Before this, the Mesozoic Era ended with one of the deadliest mass extinctions of all time. It was caused by a huge asteroid that crashed into the Earth, wiping out 75 per cent of all life, including most dinosaurs. This brought on the Cenozoic Era, also known as the Age of Mammals. Although mammals had lived alongside dinosaurs during most of the Mesozoic, the Cenozoic was when they started to dominate the planet. Many animal groups, such as whales, elephants, and primates (including humans), appeared during this time. In this section, you will meet many ancient animals that inhabited our planet before humans arrived.

The Cenozoic Era is divided into three periods:
- Paleogene (66–23 MYA) • Neogene (23–3 MYA)
- Quaternary (3 MYA–Today)

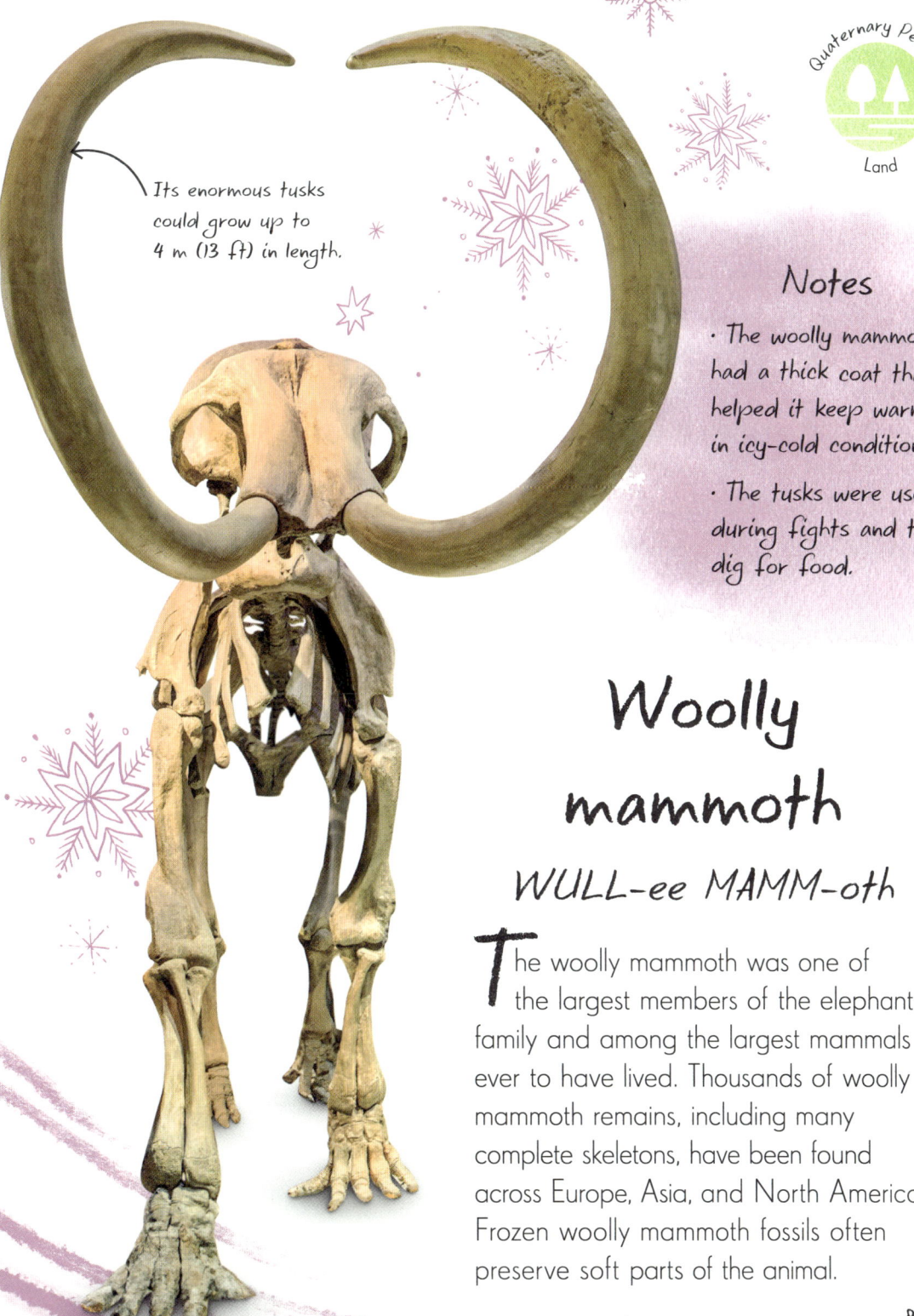

Its enormous tusks could grow up to 4 m (13 ft) in length.

Quaternary Period

Land

Notes

- The woolly mammoth had a thick coat that helped it keep warm in icy-cold conditions.
- The tusks were used during fights and to dig for food.

Woolly mammoth

WULL-ee MAMM-oth

The woolly mammoth was one of the largest members of the elephant family and among the largest mammals ever to have lived. Thousands of woolly mammoth remains, including many complete skeletons, have been found across Europe, Asia, and North America. Frozen woolly mammoth fossils often preserve soft parts of the animal.

Paleogene Period — Land, Water

Its sharp-edged teeth helped slice through fish.

Pakicetus

pah-kuh-SEE-tuhss

About the size of a wolf, Pakicetus was a walking whale. It had a thick, bony wall around its ears, four sturdy legs, and was probably covered entirely in fur. Pakicetus was a close relative of modern cetaceans, including whales, dolphins, and porpoises. It lived in what is today Pakistan and India, in Asia.

Notes

- Pakicetus spent most of its life on land, but also hunted in rivers and lakes.
- It lived around 45-50 million years ago.
- At least four different species have been identified so far.

Basilosaurus
ba-sil-oh-SOR-uss

Water

Basilosaurus is considered to be the first gigantic whale to live all of its life in water. At about 18 m (60 ft) or more in length, it was also the first giant marine top predator of its time. Many Basilosaurus fossils, including several skeletons and skulls, have been found in parts of the USA, Africa, and Peru in South America.

Its eel-like body enabled it to swim smoothly through water while hunting for many types of fish and whales.

Jagged teeth to grab big prey

Skull as long as 1.5 m (5 ft)

Paleogene Period

Land · Water

Icadyptes

eek-AH-dip-dees

The long-beaked Icadyptes was one of the largest penguins of all time. Standing 1.5 m (5 ft) tall, this extinct penguin was taller than any living species. Its only known fossils include a partial skeleton with a well-preserved skull, which was found in Peru, South America, in 2005. This early penguin seemed to have lived in a way similar to modern penguins — hunting for food in water.

Its large skull was more than 30 cm (12 in) long.

Its spear-like beak was the longest of any known penguin — almost 25 cm (10 in).

The long beak was used to strike its prey.

Ceratogaulus
seh-RAT-oh-GAWL-us

Neogene Period
Land

Ceratogaulus is the only known rodent with horns. Considered the smallest horned mammal, it had two tall horns that were quite large compared to its small body. They were probably used to fight off predators and attract mates. Most Ceratogaulus fossils have been found in Nebraska, USA.

It was about 30 cm (1 ft) long.

Ceratogaulus used its front limbs to dig.

Notes
- Ceratogaulus was an excellent digger and lived inside burrows that it made.
- Scientists used to think its horns were used for digging.

Paleogene Period — Land

Paraceratherium

PARRA-serra-THEER-ee-um

Possibly the largest mammal ever to have walked on land, Paraceratherium was an ancient type of rhinoceros that had no horns. It lived roughly during the middle part of the Cenozoic. Many of its fossils have been discovered in Asia, including giant skulls that were over 1 m (3 ft) long.

Paraceratherium was taller than a giraffe and as heavy as three elephants.

Its enormous height allowed it to reach leaves at the tops of trees.

Strong, sturdy legs helped to carry its bulky body.

Paleogene Period

Water   Land

Titanoboa

tai-tan-oh-BOH-a

Following the Cretaceous mass extinction, Titanoboa was the first super predator to roam the Earth. It is known to be the largest snake ever to have lived. All of its fossils were found in a coal mine in Colombia, South America. These included parts of the spine, ribs, and skull.

Four large neck bones

Notes

- Titanoboa lived in a tropical rainforest, which was similar to today's Amazon Rainforest.

- It would have dined on a variety of animals, including fish, turtles, and crocodiles.

Neogene Period
Water

Stupendemys

stu-PEN-dem-ees

One of the biggest turtles of all time, Stupendemys is considered the largest freshwater turtle to date. It probably lived in humid, swampy lakes and rivers, feeding on molluscs and fish. Fossils of Stupendemys have been found in Venezuela and Colombia, South America.

Notes

- The shell of a Stupendemys usually grew to a length of 2 m (7 ft) or more.

- It was named Stupendemys, meaning "stupendous turtle", after its huge size.

Shells like this one are often incomplete with many pieces missing.

The shell protected Stupendemys against predators like crocodiles.

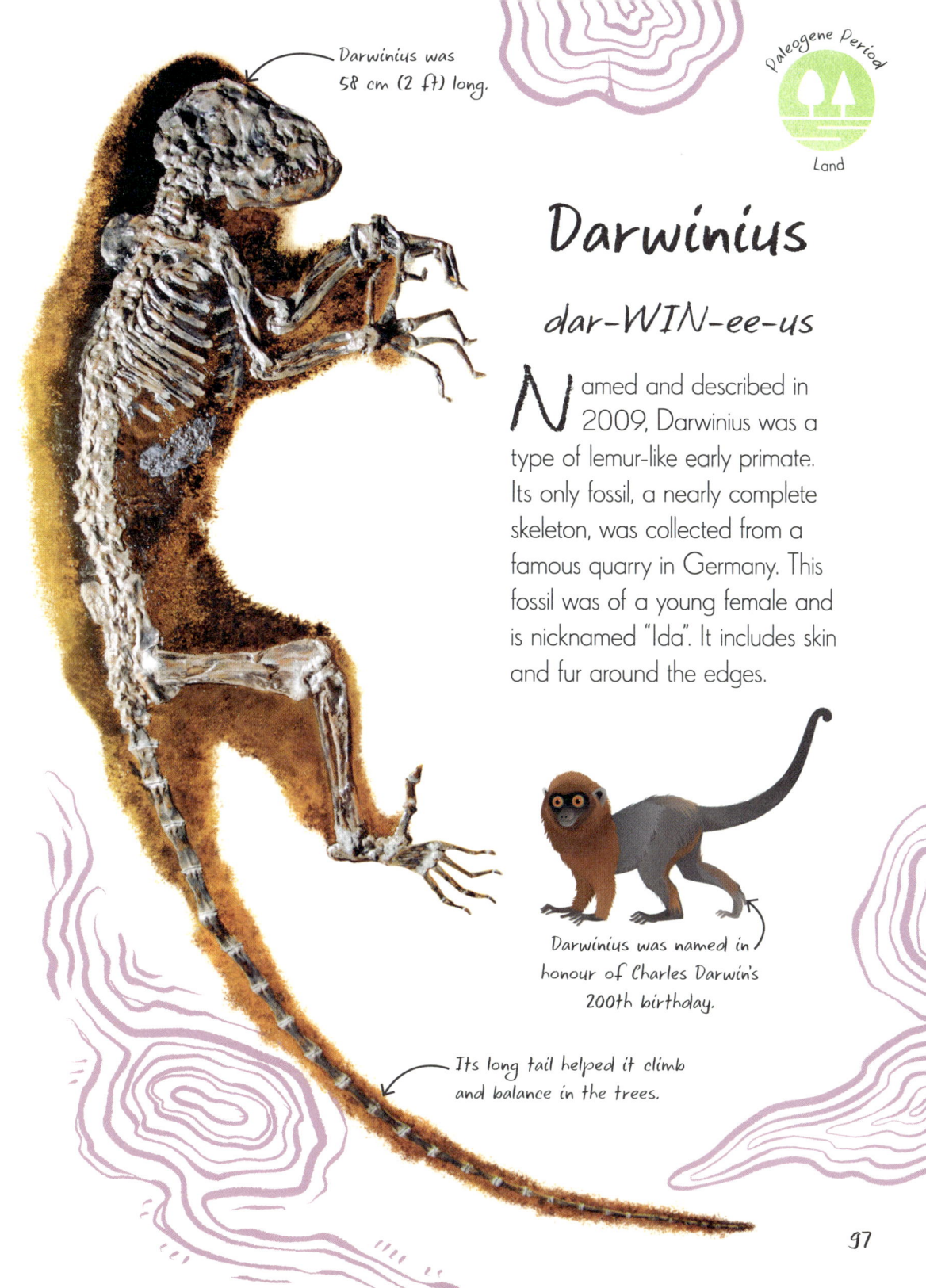

Darwinius was 58 cm (2 ft) long.

Paleogene Period
Land

Darwinius
dar-WIN-ee-us

Named and described in 2009, Darwinius was a type of lemur-like early primate. Its only fossil, a nearly complete skeleton, was collected from a famous quarry in Germany. This fossil was of a young female and is nicknamed "Ida". It includes skin and fur around the edges.

Darwinius was named in honour of Charles Darwin's 200th birthday.

Its long tail helped it climb and balance in the trees.

Famous fossil sites

Some fossil sites preserve details of soft parts, including skin and fur. Others may contain bone beds with thousands of fossils. Studying fossil sites like these can help paleontologists learn more about where prehistoric animals lived.

Animal remains at Ashfall Fossil Beds

Volcanic site

Ashfall Fossil Beds is a 12-million-year-old site in Nebraska, USA. Many well-preserved skeletons of animals that had gathered around an ancient watering hole were found there. These animals, including rhinos, camels, and turtles, were killed by deadly ash from a volcanic eruption.

Dinosaur bone beds

Some of the most complete dinosaur fossils, such as those of Stegosaurus, Diplodocus, and Allosaurus, were found in the famous Morrison Formation. This vast rock unit extends through western USA and is home to bone beds of many dinosaurs that lived during the Late Jurassic.

Dinosaur fossils from the Morrison Formation

Early breeding ground

Thousands of ichthyosaur remains have been found in many quarries near the town of Holzmaden, Germany. Of these, more than 100 fossils were of pregnant ichthyosaurs. This area appears to have been an Early Jurassic breeding ground.

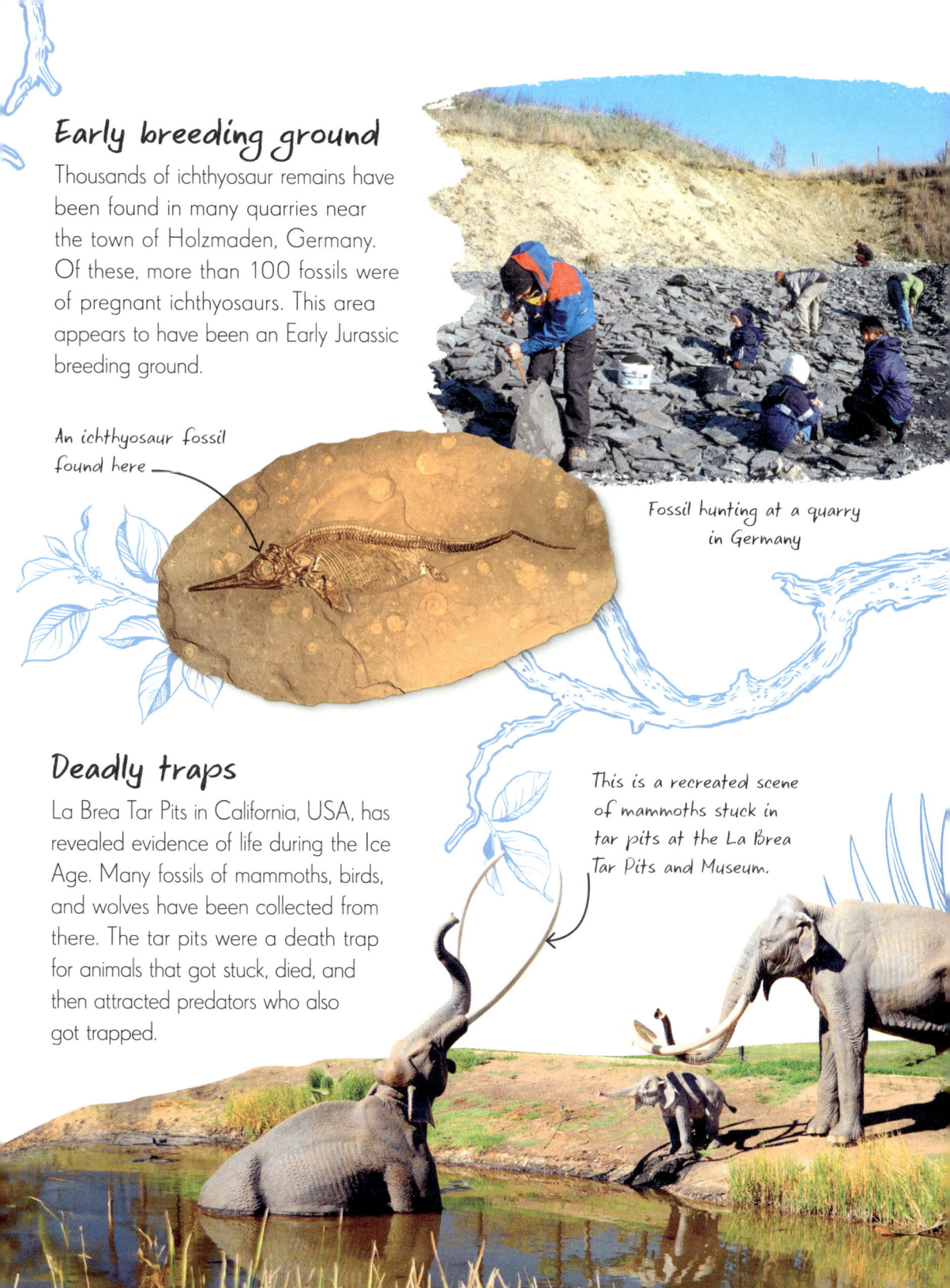

Fossil hunting at a quarry in Germany

An ichthyosaur fossil found here

Deadly traps

La Brea Tar Pits in California, USA, has revealed evidence of life during the Ice Age. Many fossils of mammoths, birds, and wolves have been collected from there. The tar pits were a death trap for animals that got stuck, died, and then attracted predators who also got trapped.

This is a recreated scene of mammoths stuck in tar pits at the La Brea Tar Pits and Museum.

Paleogene Period — Land

Sifrhippus
siff-RIP-uss

Sifrhippus was a tiny, prehistoric horse, which was about the size of a house cat. It lived in herds and spent most of its time in forests. As the climate warmed over thousands of years, Sifrhippus shrank in size. Almost every Sifrhippus fossil comes from Wyoming, USA, and includes many bones and teeth.

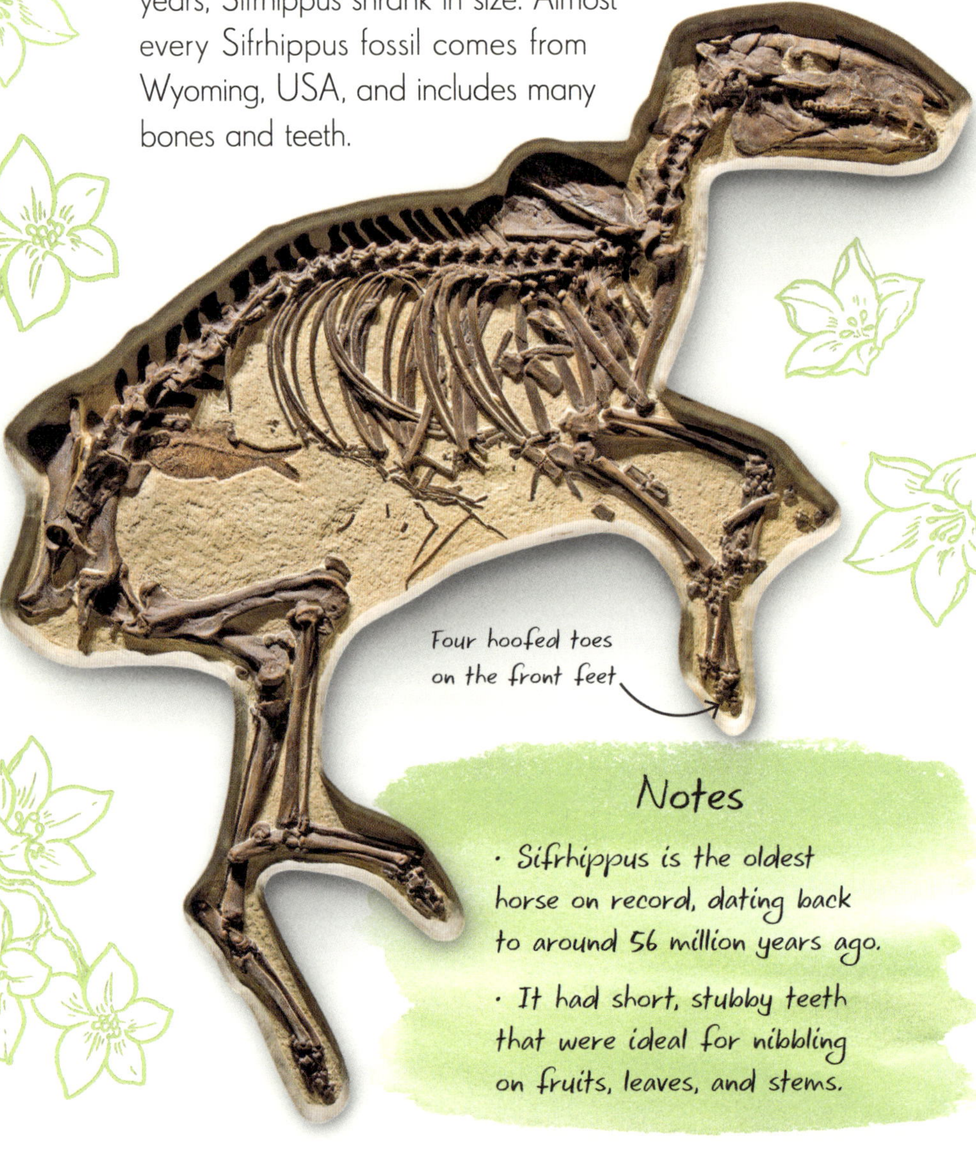

Four hoofed toes on the front feet.

Notes

- Sifrhippus is the oldest horse on record, dating back to around 56 million years ago.
- It had short, stubby teeth that were ideal for nibbling on fruits, leaves, and stems.

Procoptodon

pro-COP-toe-don

Quaternary Period — Land

Named in 1874, Procoptodon was an ancient kangaroo. The largest and heaviest kangaroo on record, *Procoptodon goliah*, was 2 m (7 ft) tall and weighed up to 240 kg (530 lb). Many Procoptodon fossils, including skulls and complete skeletons, have been found at many sites across Australia.

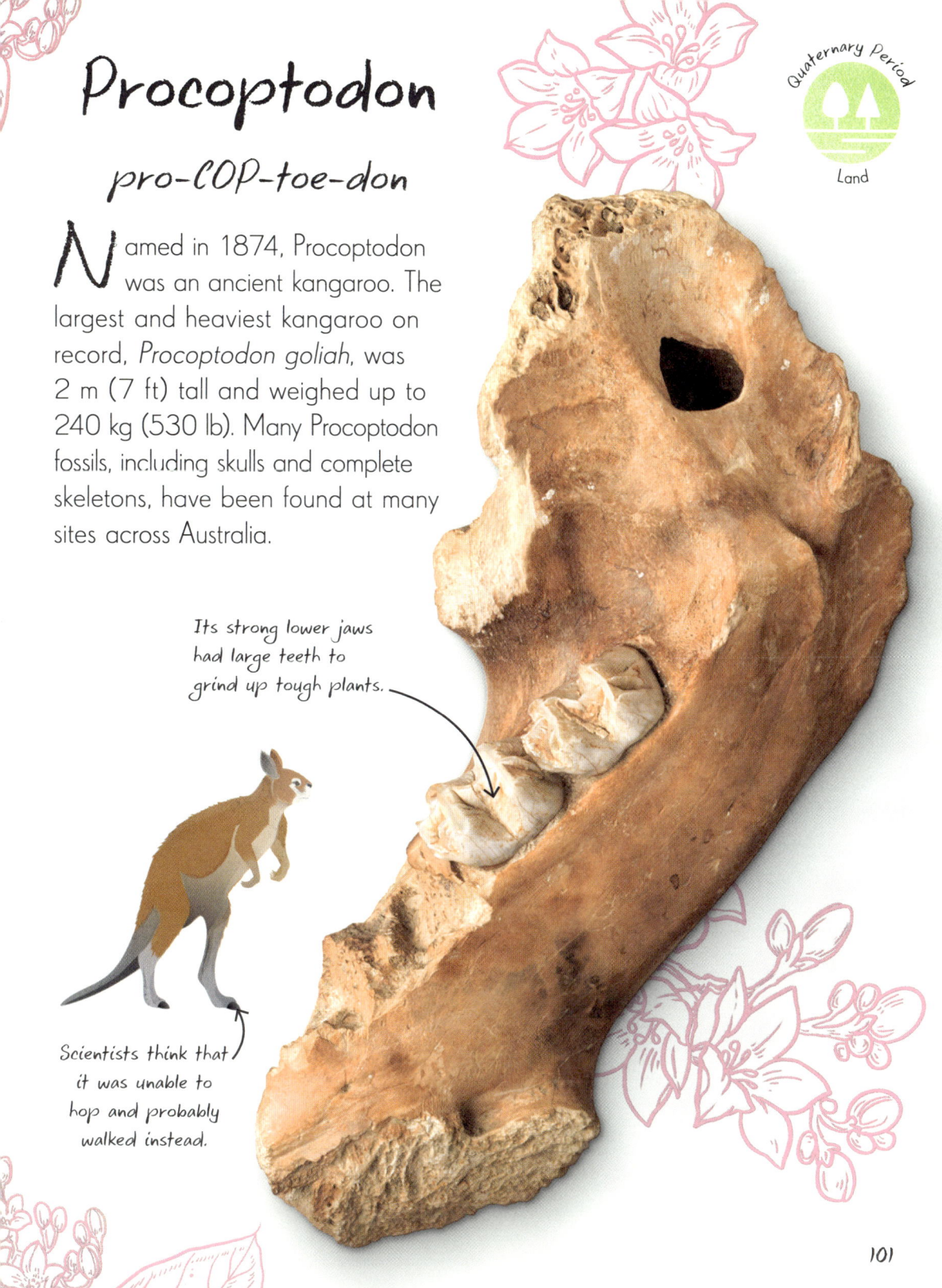

Its strong lower jaws had large teeth to grind up tough plants.

Scientists think that it was unable to hop and probably walked instead.

Paleogene Period

Land · Air

It had a long tail, unlike modern bats.

Claws on each finger and short, broad wings suggest it was capable of short flights.

Icaronycteris

ICK-ah-roe-NICK-teh-riss

Taking to the skies about 52 million years ago, Icaronycteris is among the oldest known bats. Complete fossils of Icaronycteris, along with two related species, were found in the Green River Formation in Wyoming, USA. This was a remarkable discovery as it is quite rare to find complete fossil bats.

Titanomyrma

tai-tan-oh-MER-ma

Titanomyrma, meaning "Ant Titan", is the perfect name for the largest ant known to have existed. Called *Titanomyrma gigantea*, this giant ant was as big as a hummingbird. Several well-preserved fossils, including complete ones, have been discovered in Germany, parts of Canada, and Wyoming in the USA.

Land

Air

Paleogene Period

Notes

- Titanomyrma was named in 2011.
- Its fossils show that it did not have a sting.
- The queens of Titanomyrma gigantea grew up to 7 cm (3 in) long, double the size of the males.

Wingspan of about 16 cm (6 in)

Some fossils show beautiful details on the wings.

Cretaceous Period–Today
Land

Platanus
PLAT-uh-nuhss

The earliest family members of Platanus, or the plane tree, go back to the Cretaceous Period. However, many of the best-known fossils belong to a later period, the Paleogene. The remains include large, often beautifully preserved leaves with incredible details. Modern plane trees are native to the northern hemisphere and may grow to heights of up to 50 m (164 ft).

Many fossil leaves show details of veins.

Slightly jagged edges

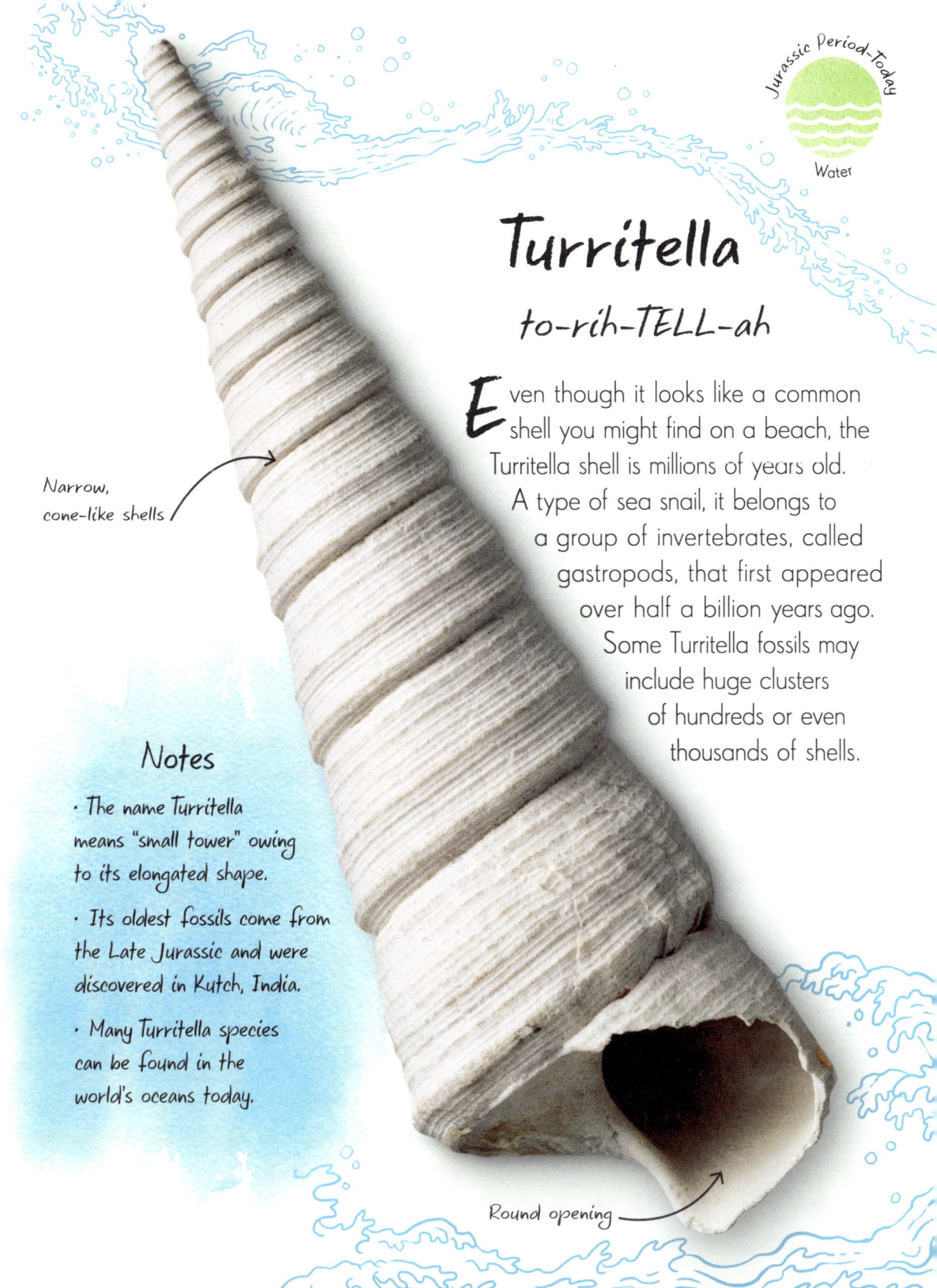

Jurassic Period-Today

Water

Turritella

to-rih-TELL-ah

Even though it looks like a common shell you might find on a beach, the Turritella shell is millions of years old. A type of sea snail, it belongs to a group of invertebrates, called gastropods, that first appeared over half a billion years ago. Some Turritella fossils may include huge clusters of hundreds or even thousands of shells.

Narrow, cone-like shells

Notes

- The name Turritella means "small tower" owing to its elongated shape.
- Its oldest fossils come from the Late Jurassic and were discovered in Kutch, India.
- Many Turritella species can be found in the world's oceans today.

Round opening

Neogene Period — Land

Its teeth could crack open the bones of its prey.

Large, domed skull

Borophagus
BOR-oaf-ag-us

Weighing about 40 kg (88 lb), Borophagus was a powerful, wolf-sized dog. It was the last surviving member of an extinct group known as the "bone-crushing dogs". These dogs were very common across North America for over 30 million years until the last members, like Borophagus, went extinct a little under 2 million years ago.

Notes

- Evidence suggests that Borophagus probably lived in packs.

- Fossilized poo found in California, USA, includes crunched-up bones of many animals it preyed on.

Archaeotherium

ar-kee-oh-theer-ee-um

Land

Nicknamed "hell pig", Archaeotherium was actually a close relative of hippos and whales. Archaeotherium would hunt early camels, among other animals, then pile up its kill in a place to eat later. Evidence of this can be found in one fossil deposit from Wyoming, USA, that contained at least seven ancient camels with bite marks similar to that of an Archaeotherium.

The cow-sized Archaeotherium looked similar to an enormous pig.

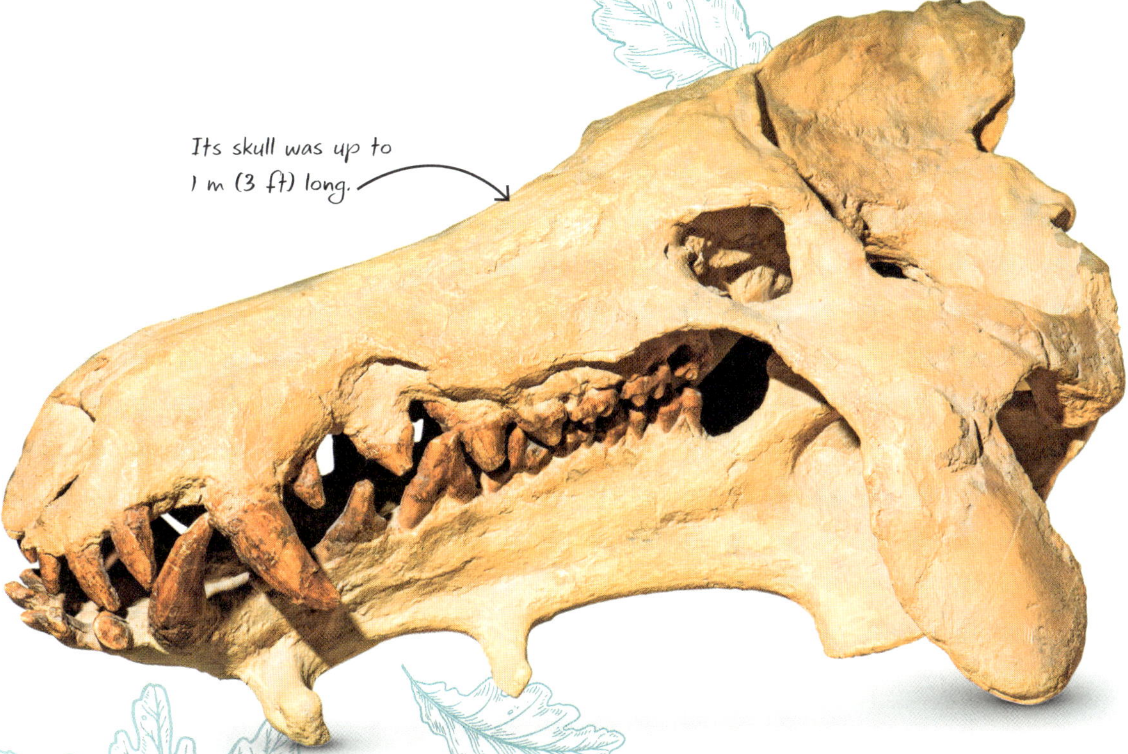

Its skull was up to 1 m (3 ft) long.

Neogene Period — Land

Strong teeth at the back of the mouth suggest it ground up tough plants.

Two long, upper tusks

The lower tusks were shorter than the upper ones.

Gomphotherium probably lived in herds, like modern elephants.

Gomphotherium

GOM-foe-THEE-ree-um

Gomphotherium belonged to an ancient group of elephant relatives called gomphotheres that first appeared almost 30 million years ago. Meaning "welded beast", it was named after its long, straight tusks. The tusks were used for digging, defence, and display. Its fossils have been found in Africa, Asia, Europe, and North America.

Mastodon

MASS-toe-don

Neogene-Quaternary Periods
Land

A cousin of gomphotheres, mastodon also belonged to an extinct family of elephants. The largest mastodon species might have weighed 9 tonnes (10 tons) — heavier than the average living African elephant. Fossils of its most famous species, the American mastodon, have been found throughout North America.

The giant tusks curved upwards.

Notes

- To maintain its enormous size, mastodon ate lots of vegetation, including fruits, twigs, and leaves.
- Many skeletons, skulls, and isolated bones have been collected.

Neogene Period
Land

Phorusrhacos
FOR-rus-RAH-kos

Phorusrhacos is the most famous member of a family of large, carnivorous birds known as "terror birds". Standing tall at about 2.5 m (8 ft), it had a giant head that was at least 60 cm (24 in) long. This speedy hunter could hit a top speed of 50 kph (30 mph), outrunning almost any prey.

Phorusrhacos may have used the sharp claws on its wings during combat.

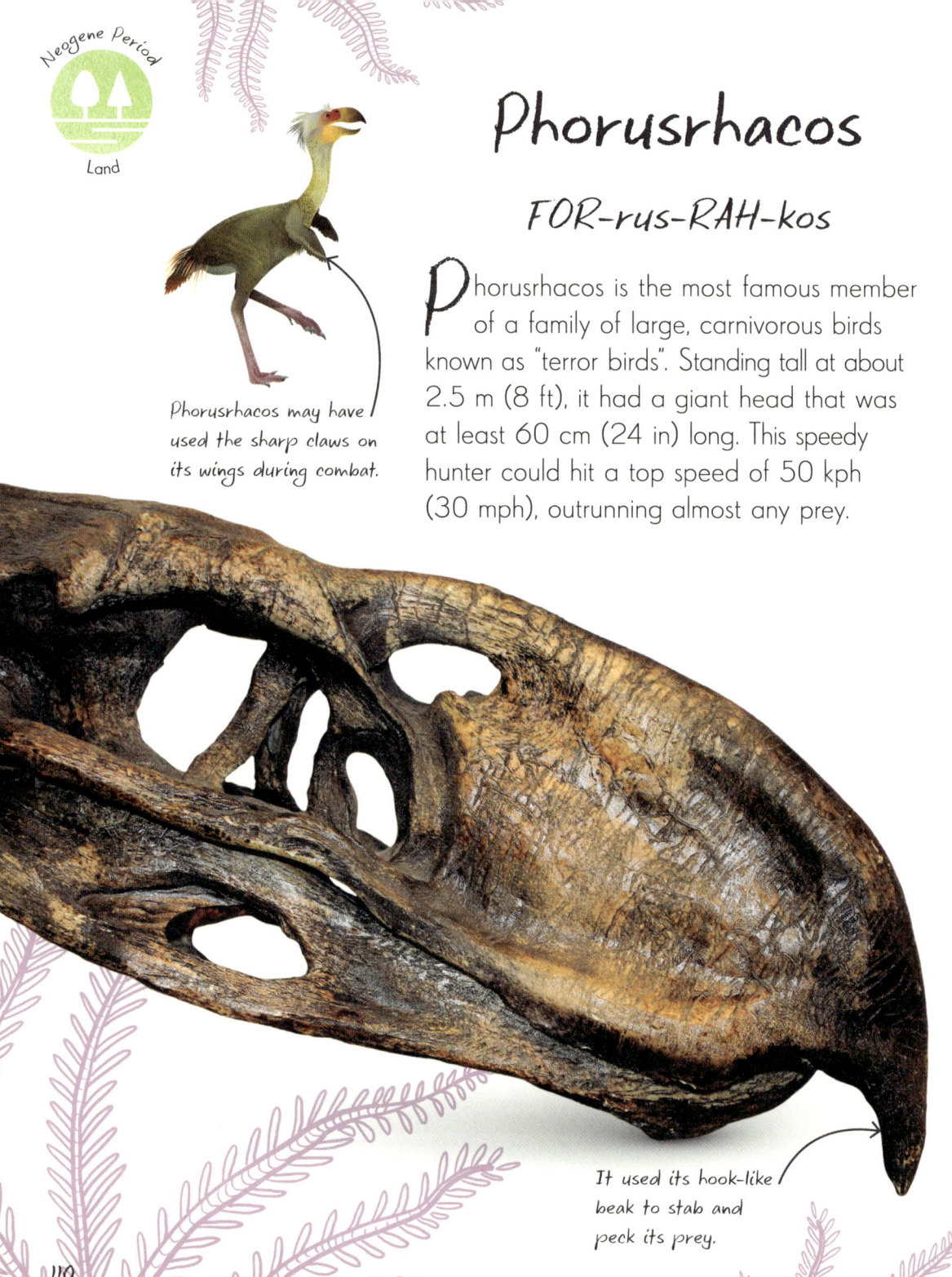

It used its hook-like beak to stab and peck its prey.

The upturned mouth suggests that it hunted smaller fish swimming just below the water's surface.

Paleogene Period

Water

Its delicately preserved fossils are usually 10 cm (4 in) long.

Diplomystus

DIP-low-MY-STUSS

An extinct relative of modern-day herring (a type of fish), Diplomystus is one of the most common fossils collected from the Green River Formation, USA. Some Diplomystus fossils have been found with fish stuck in their mouth, whereas others have been unearthed with the last meals preserved.

Notes

- Scientists have found evidence that suggests Rodoldelphis ate fish and not marine mammals, unlike its modern cousins.

- Rodoldelphis was around 5 m (17 ft) long.

Large jaws with thick, curved teeth

Rododelphis

row-doh-DEL-fiss

In 2020, fossil expert Polychronis Stamatiadis discovered a rare partial skeleton on the island of Rhodes, Greece. This one-of-a-kind fossil belonged to a false killer whale, which was closely related to modern false killer whales and killer whales. In 2022, it was identified as a new species and named *Rododelphis stamatiadisi* after its discoverer.

Otodus megalodon
Oh-TOH-dus MEG-uh-lo-DON

Neogene Period
Water

Commonly known as megalodon, this shark was one of the largest and deadliest predators to have ever lived. It measured up to 18 m (59 ft) in length. Countless megalodon teeth have been found worldwide and some of them are up to 18 cm (7 in) long. This is how it got its name, which means "big tooth".

Megalodon had rows of up to 300 triangular teeth in its jaws.

The triangle-shaped tooth could slice through prey.

Land

Doedicurus was a herbivore and ate low-growing plants, including leaves, berries, and grasses.

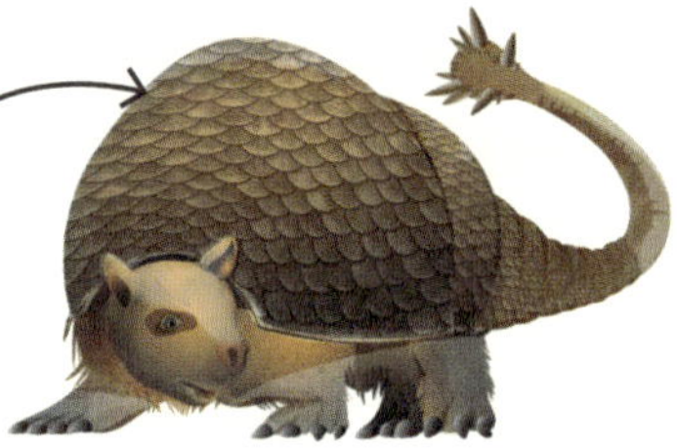

Doedicurus

doh-dih-KER-uss

Measuring the size of a small car, the hefty Doedicurus belonged to an extinct family of armadillos called glyptodonts. Scientists believe that it may have swung its deadly tail club as a form of defence. Fossils of Doedicurus, including complete skeletons, have been found in North and South America.

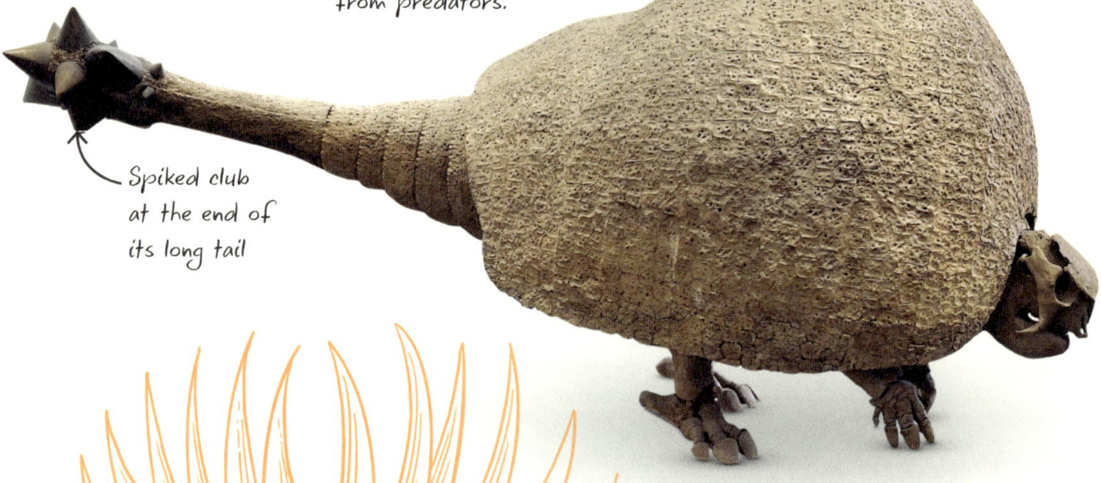

Its tough, domed shell protected it from predators.

Spiked club at the end of its long tail

Smilodon

Quaternary Period
Land

SMILE-oh-don

Smilodon was a sabre-toothed cat that had huge canine teeth to pierce through its prey. About the size of a tiger but with a muscular, bear-like build, Smilodon was one of the most fearsome predators of its time. It would have dined on many animals, such as deer, horse, and mammoths.

Notes

- Smilodon fossils have been found in North and South America.
- It lived between 10,000 and 2.5 million years ago.

Its two large canine teeth grew to almost 30 cm (12 in) long.

It used its powerful limbs to grip and hold prey.

Neogene-Quaternary Periods — Land

Megatherium
MEG-ah-THEER-ee-um

Elephant-sized Megatherium was a huge sloth that reached about 6 m (20 ft) in length. Unlike living sloths that live in trees, Megatherium spent all of its life on the ground. Its fossils have especially been found in the Pampas region of Argentina, and reveal that it lived between 10,000 and 100,000 years ago.

Massive skull

Short, bulky legs

Notes

- Charles Darwin found Megatherium fossils during his voyage aboard the HMS Beagle.

- Giant ground sloths dug huge underground burrows and lived inside them.

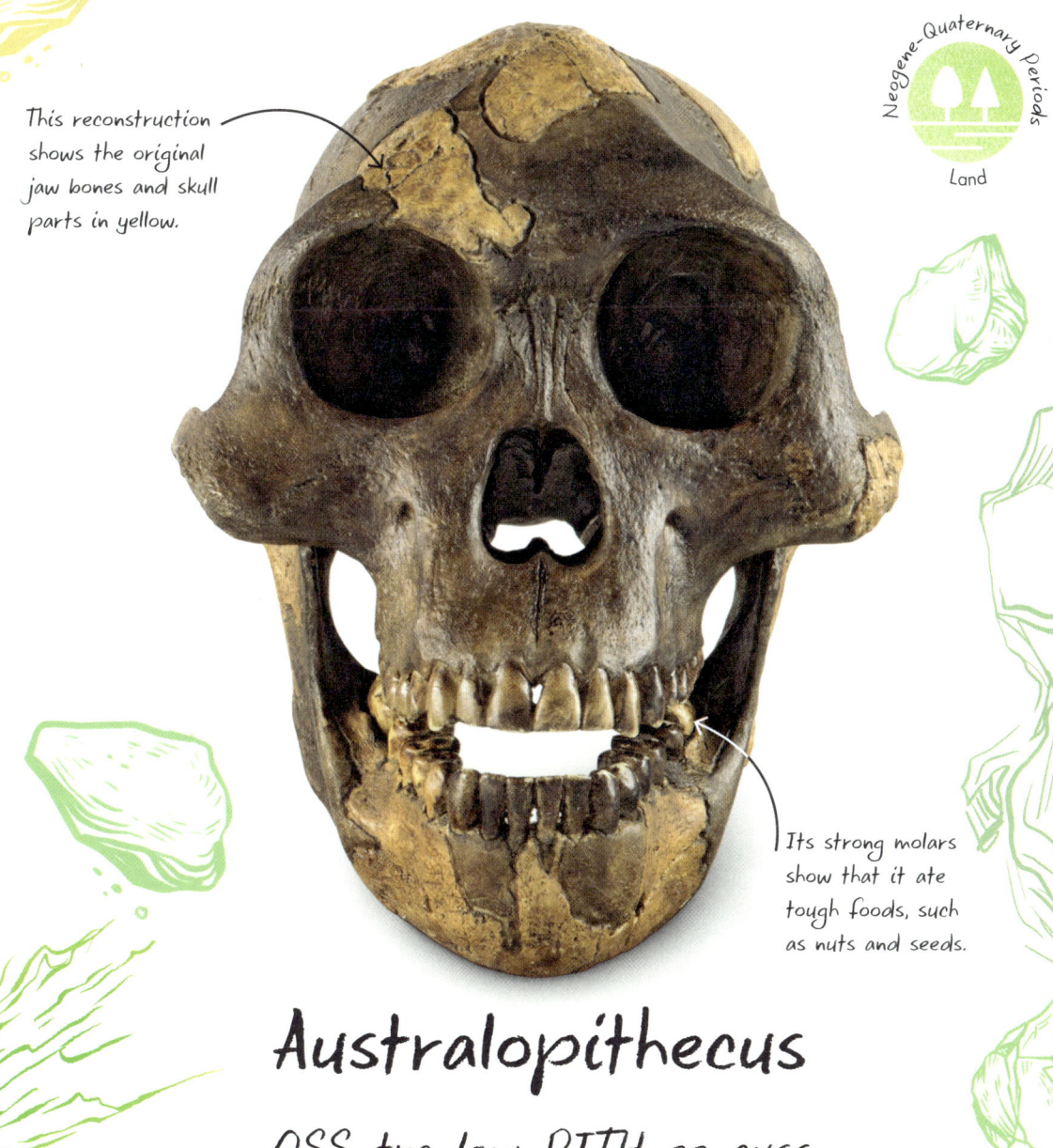

This reconstruction shows the original jaw bones and skull parts in yellow.

Neogene-Quaternary Periods
Land

Its strong molars show that it ate tough foods, such as nuts and seeds.

Australopithecus

OSS-tra-low-PITH-ee-cuss

Perhaps the most famous relative of humans, Australopithecus walked upright on two legs. It had a mixture of ape-like and human-like features. All its fossils come from Africa. The most famous fossil find is the partial skeleton of a young female, nicknamed "Lucy".

Fossil finders

For over 200 years, paleontologists have been studying fossils. From Mary Anning's ichthyosaur and plesiosaur finds to Richard Owen, who coined the word "dinosaur", many historic scientists have contributed to this field. Today, paleontologists work in museums, universities, laboratories, and many other places.

Joan Wiffen

Dr Joan Wiffen was a self-taught and well-known scientist. She was one of New Zealand's leading paleontologists, who discovered and described many fossils, including the first dinosaurs from New Zealand.

Lindsay Zanno

An American paleontologist, Dr Lindsay Zanno has led expeditions all over the world, discovering and describing many new dinosaur species. She has been encouraging people of all ages to explore paleontology. She is also one of the world's leading experts on theropods.

Dean Lomax

Dr Dean Lomax is a British paleontologist, author, TV host, and science communicator. A leading expert on ichthyosaurs, he has named several species and led many excavations around the world.

Karen Chin

Dr Karen Chin is an American scientist who is one of the world's leading experts in coprolites (fossilized poo). She is known to be the first paleontologist to identify a giant T. rex coprolite.

Dr Lomax with an ichthyosaur fossil

Professor Xu Xing at a fossil site in China.

Xu Xing

Professor Xu Xing has named more dinosaurs than anybody else — over 80 species. A renowned Chinese paleontologist, he has led new research, especially on Chinese dinosaurs, birds, and other fossils.

A dinosaur dig

One of the most exciting tasks of a paleontologist is digging out (or excavating) the ancient remains of an animal that no one has ever seen before. Once a fossil is found, it is carefully collected, cleaned, and studied to discover more about prehistoric life.

Digging for fossils

Depending on where the fossil was located and other factors, such as the weather, it may take weeks, months, or even years to complete a dig. Paleontologists use various tools to chip away the rock around the fossil, including hammers, chisels, and trowels.

A paleontologist looking for fossils at a site.

Handling with care

If the bones are large, heavy, or fragile, they can be wrapped in plaster, paper tissues, and fabric to protect them from damage. Once the plaster hardens, the fossil can be carefully removed and sent to a laboratory to be studied.

Plaster helps prevent loss of important information.

Cleaning the fossil

After a fossil has been fully removed from the ground, the team inspects the area to ensure no loose bones are lost. In the lab, drills and other tools are then used to separate rock from bone. This process may take several years to complete.

Unusual finds

Not all dinosaur digs focus on big bones and teeth. Sometimes, you might find rare or delicate fossils, such as "Baby Yingliang". Collected in southern China, this was one of the best dinosaur embryos ever found, perfectly preserved inside an egg.

Can you find a fossil?

Yes, you can! Fossil hunting can be a thrilling adventure. Fossils are found around the world — from mountains or deserts to beaches, or sometimes even in your gardens! All you need to know is what to look for and how to collect them safely.

Getting started

Before visiting a fossil site, it is important to plan ahead and do some research. Read books and look at photos of fossils to understand what to look for. If you do not find any fossils, or discover just a few parts, do not feel discouraged. Fossil hunting is a skill that takes time.

Safety first

• Always get permission before visiting a fossil site.

• Make sure you are allowed to collect fossils.

• Always take an adult with you.

• Avoid cliffs and going near roads. At beaches and rivers, watch out for slippery rocks and rising water levels.

• Make sure to wear safety gear, such as a helmet and gloves, when needed.

Caring for fossils

Hurrah! You have found a fossil. Make sure to keep your finds safe inside clear bags, trays, drawers, or wooden boxes. You could also display them on a shelf or in a cabinet. When handling fossils, always use both hands to prevent damage.

Fossil collection in a drawer

Thinking like a scientist

Just like paleontologists, make sure you record all the key information about the fossil — where it was found, date, location, and fossil type. This ensures that the history of the fossil is not lost.

Glossary

amber
Fossilized tree resin that may contain the remains of plants and animals from millions of years ago

ambush
Surprise attack

ammonite
Ancient marine animal that usually had a spiral shell. Related to modern squid and octopuses

amphibian
Cold-blooded animal that can live both on land and in water, such as frogs

ancestor
Ancient relative

armour
Protective layer or shell that covers an animal, such as the hard scales of an alligator

arthropod
Invertebrate with a hard outer skeleton and a segmented body, such as a woodlouse (see invertebrate)

asteroid
Rocky object that orbits the Sun

bacteria
Tiny, single-celled living things that can be found almost everywhere on Earth

bone bed
Layer of earth where many animal bones are found together

brachiopod
Soft-bodied marine animal with no backbone and two joined shells that mirror each other

carnivore
Any animal that eats other animals for food

ceratopsian
Plant-eating dinosaur with enormous horns and bony frills, such as Triceratops

coprolite
Fossilized poo. It can contain traces of an animal's last meal

crest
Raised part on the head of an animal, including a bird or dinosaur

describing (a fossil)
Providing details of the features of a fossil, such as size, shape, and type

dinosaur
Reptile that appeared millions of years ago, long before people existed. All dinosaurs lived on land, although some could fly and others could swim

embryo
Early stage of development of an animal or plant, before its organs are fully formed

era
An era is divided into many shorter periods

evolution
Process where living things change, over many generations, and may become new species

extinction
Dying out of a species

fossil
Preserved remains or traces of a once-living animal or plant

fossilization
Process where a plant or animal gets preserved over a long time and turns into a fossil. It takes thousands to millions of years

gastropod
Mollusc that has a one-piece shell, or a related mollusc such as a slug (see mollusc)

Ice Age
Long period of time, thousands of years ago, when large parts of the Earth's surface were covered in ice

ichthyosaur
Type of marine reptile, some of which resembled dolphins. Ichthyosaurs lived during the Mesozoic Era

invertebrate
Animal with no backbone

mammal
Any animal that gives birth to live young and feeds them on milk, such as dogs or bears

mollusc
Soft-bodied and boneless animal, which often has a hard shell

multicellular
Organism with many cells

paleontologist
Scientist who studies the history of life on Earth, usually by examining fossils

period
A long span of time that lasts millions of years. Many periods make up an era

plankton
Very tiny plants and animals that live in water

plesiosaur
Type of marine reptile that varied in appearance, including pliosaurs, which had giant heads with big teeth, and elasmosaurs, which had extremely long necks

pollen
Fine, powdery grains that animals carry from flower to flower, so that the flower can produce seeds

predator
Animal that eats other animals for food

preserve
Keep something the same or prevent it from being damaged

prey
Animal that is hunted and killed by another for food

proboscis
Long, tube-like mouthpart that some insects, such as butterflies, have. They use it to suck up food, such as nectar

pterosaur
Group of flying reptiles that were the first vertebrates capable of flight. They lived throughout the Mesozoic Era (see vertebrate)

radioactive
Object that may give off harmful rays or radiation. In fossils, radioactive elements are studied to understand the age of the rocks

reconstruct
Recreation of something from the past

reptile
Cold-blooded, scaly vertebrate, such as crocodiles, snakes, and turtles. It usually lays soft-shelled eggs on land

tentacles
Long, soft body parts that some animals use to grasp or feed, such as octopuses or jellyfish

sail
Tall structure on a dinosaur's back, made of long bones, which looks like a sail on a boat

sauropod
Group of dinosaurs with long necks and tails, which includes the largest animals ever to have walked on Earth

species
Type of plant or animal with shared features, which can usually reproduce with members of the same species

specimen
Individual or object that represents an example of its species

tetrapod
Animal with four legs or limbs, such as mammals, birds, reptiles, and amphibians

theropod
Group of predatory dinosaurs with sharp teeth and claws. They are now represented by all living birds

trilobite
Type of marine arthropod with a body divided into three sections

tusk
Long tooth that grows from the jaws of animals, such as elephants and mammoths

venomous
Substance that may be deadly if an animal or plant injects it through a sting or fangs

vertebrate
Animal that has a backbone or spine

wingspan
Distance between the two tips of a pair of wings

Index

A
Age of Mammals 88
Age of Plants 28
Alasemenia 27
Albertonectes 58
Allosaurus 68, 98
amber 9, 57
ammonites 60
amphibians 40
ankylosaurs 73
Ankylosaurus 86
Anning, Mary 52, 118
Anomalocaris 13
ants 103
Araucaria 78
Archaeopteryx 74
Archaeotherium 107
Argentinosaurus 54
Arizonasaurus 47
armadillos 114
Arthropleura 33
arthropods 14, 33
Ashfall Fossil Beds (USA) 98
Aspidorhynchus 65
Australopithecus 117
Aviculopecten 19

B
babies 55, 66, 71, 81
bacteria 10, 11
Basilosaurus 91
bats 102
behaviour 64–65
belemnites 61
birds 67, 74, 110
bivalves 19
body fossils 8–9
bones 8
Borophagus 106
brachiopods 18
breeding grounds 99
Burgess Shale (Canada) 13, 22–23
burial 6

C
Cambrian Period 12, 22
Cantabrigiaster 24
Carboniferous Period 12, 25, 28
carnivores 41, 62, 110
Carnotaurus 83
Cenozoic Era 10, 88, 94
Ceratogaulus 93
ceratopsians 80, 86

cetaceans 90
chimaeras 37
Chin, Karen 119
claws 14, 54, 64, 68, 74, 84, 102, 110
clubs, tail 73, 114
coal 29
coelacanths 35
cold-water reefs 24
colour 55
Confuciusornis 67
Cooksonia 26
coprolites 8, 106
coral 20, 21
crabs 57
crests 62, 63, 81
Cretaceous mass extinction 95
Cretaceous Period 44, 50, 59, 66, 70, 75, 76, 79, 83, 86, 87, 104
Cretapsara 57
crinoids 25, 51
crocodilians 47, 82
Cryolophosaurus 62

D
Darwin, Charles 97, 116
Darwinius 97
dating fossils 10–11
death 6
Deinosuchus 82
Dendromaia 29
Devonian Period 12, 38, 39
Didymograptus 30
Dimetrodon 42
dinosaurs 7, 8, 44, 45, 46, 50, 54, 55, 62–65, 68–69, 71–74, 78, 80–81, 83–87, 88, 98, 118, 119
Diplodocus 69, 98
Diplomystus 111
Doedicurus 114
dogs 106
Dunkleosteus 36

E
echinoderms 24
eggs 64, 71
elephants 89, 108, 109
embryos 55
eras 10
erosion 7
Eurypterus 17
evolution 7

F
feathers 55, 67, 74
fights 64
filter feeders 18
fins 34, 35, 39, 56
fish 34–39, 56, 65, 76, 111
flowering plants 44, 79
food 65, 76, 111
footprints 9, 65
fossil hunting 7, 118–121
fossil sites, famous 98–99
fossil types 8–9
fossilization 6–7
frills 80, 86

G
gastropods 25
geological time 10
gills 34, 57
ginkgo 50
glyptodonts 114
Gomphotherium 108
graptolites 30
griffenflies 32

H
hadrosaurs 71, 81
Haikouichthys 34
Hallucigenia 23
Halysites 20
Helicoprion 37
Heliophyllum 21
herds 65
Herrerasaurus 46
Hesperornithoides 68
Hildoceras 60
Holzmaden (Germany) 99
horns 63, 80, 83, 86, 93
horses 100
humans 117

I
Icadyptes 92
Icaronycteris 102
Ice Age 9, 99
ichthyosaurs 44, 52, 53, 99, 118, 119
Ichthyosaurus 52
Ichthyotitan 53
Inostrancevia 41
Isotelus 16

J
Jaekelopterus 17
jawed fish 36
Jurassic Period 44, 50, 51, 60, 63, 69, 98, 99, 105

K
kangaroos 101
Keichousaurus 55
Kronosaurus 59
Kunmingella 64

L
La Brea Tar Pits (USA) 99
Leedsichthys 56
Lepidodendron 29
limbs 39
Lisowicia 49
Lokiceratops 80
Lomax, Dean 52, 68, 119
Lystrosaurus 43

M
Magnolia 79
Maiasaura 71
mammals 41, 44, 49, 70, 88
mammoths 9, 89, 99
marine reptiles 7, 44, 52, 53, 55, 58, 77
mass extinctions 43, 88, 95
mastodon 109
Mastodonsaurus 40
Meganeura 32
Megateuthis 61
Megatherium 116
Mesozoic Era 10, 44, 88
millipedes 33
mineralization 7
Miragaia 72
molluscs 19, 25, 44
Morrison Formation (USA) 98
mosasaurs 77
multicellular organisms 11
Myllokunmingia 34

N
Neogene Period 88
nests 8, 71
Ngamugawi 35

O
Opabinia 14
Ordovician Period 12
Otodus megalodon 113
Ottoia 15
Owen, Richard 118

P
Pachycephalosaurus 87
Pakicetus 90
paleoethology 64
Paleozoic Era 10, 12
Paleogene Period 88, 104
paleontologists 6, 118–119
Paraceratherium 94
Parasaurolophus 11, 81
parenting 64, 71
Pecopteris 28
penguins 92
periods 10
permafrost 9
Permian Period 12, 18, 43
Permo–Triassic extinction 43
Phorusrhacos 110
placoderms 36
Platanus 104
Platyceras 25
plesiosaurs 58, 59
pliosaurs 59
pollen 7, 79
poo 8, 106
potassium 10
priapulids 15
proboscis 14
Proceratosaurus 63
Procoptodon 101
Protoceratops 64
Pterodaustro 66
pterosaurs 44, 65, 66
Pugnax 18

Q
Quaternary Period 88
Quetzalcoatlus 75

R
radiometric dating 10
record breakers 54–55
Repenomamus 70
resin 9
Rhamphorhynchus 65
rodents 93
Rododelphis 112
rostrum 61

S
sabre-toothed cats 115
safety 120
sails 42, 47, 85
sea scorpions 17
sea snails 105
sea stars 24
sediment 6, 7
Seirocrinus 51
sharks 38, 113
Shonisaurus 55
Sifrhippus 100
Silurian Period 12, 25
single-celled organisms 11
Sinosauropteryx 55
skeletons 7, 8
slime 11
sloths 116
Smilodon 115
Spinosaurus 85
sporangium 26
Spriggina 11
Stegoceras 8
Stegosaurus 68, 72, 98
stromatolites 10, 11
Stupendemys 96
Supersaurus 69

T
Tanystropheus 48
teeth 8
tetrapods 39
Therizinosaurus 54
theropods 54, 62, 83, 85
Tiktaalik 39
Titanoboa 95
Titanomyrma 103
tooth whorls 37
trace fossils 8, 9
tracks 8, 9, 65
Triassic Period 38, 43, 44, 49, 53, 55
Triceratops 80, 86
trilobiltes 16
Turritella 105
turtles 96
tusks 89, 108
Tylosaurus 77
tyrannosaurs 63
Tyrannosaurus rex 45, 63, 86

V
Vaderlimulus 31
Velociraptor 64, 68, 84
vertebrates 35
volcanic eruptions 98

W
Walcott, Charles Doolittle 22, 23
Waptia fieldensis 23
whales 90, 91, 112
Wiffen, Joan 118
winged seeds 27
wings 84
Wiwaxia 23
woolly mammoths 9, 89

X
Xenacanthus 38
Xiphactinus 76
Xu Xing 119

Z
Zanno, Lindsay 118
zooids 30
Zuul 73

The authorised representative in the EEA is
Dorling Kindersley Verlag GmbH. Arnulfstr. 124,
80636 Munich, Germany

Copyright © 2025 Dorling Kindersley Limited
A Penguin Random House Company
10 9 8 7 6 5 4 3 2 1
001–345733–Sept/2025

All rights reserved.
No part of this publication may be reproduced, stored in or introduced into a retrieval system, or transmitted, in any form, or by any means (electronic, mechanical, photocopying, recording, or otherwise), without the prior written permission of the copyright owner.
No part of this publication may be used or reproduced in any manner for the purpose of training artificial intelligence technologies or systems. In accordance with Article 4(3)of the DSM Directive 2019/790, DK expressly reserves this work from the text and data mining exception.

A CIP catalogue record for this book
is available from the British Library.
ISBN: 978-0-2417-2526-9
Printed and bound in China

www.dk.com

Senior editor Radhika Haswani
Project editor Srijani Ganguly
Project art editor Bhagyashree Nayak
Art editor Nishtha Gupta
Assistant art editor Shaarang Bhanot
Pre-production image editor Ashok Kumar
Pre-production coordinator Vishal Bhatia
Senior picture researcher Deepak Negi
Senior jacket designer Rashika Kachroo
Managing editor Roohi Sehgal
Managing art editors Elle Ward, Ivy Sengupta
Production editor Anita Yadav
Production controller Jack Matts
Delhi creative head Malavika Talukder
Associate publisher Gemma Farr
Art director Mabel Chan

Editorial consultant Steve Hoffman

First published in Great Britain in 2025 by
Dorling Kindersley Limited
20 Vauxhall Bridge Road,
London SW1V 2SA

This book was made with Forest Stewardship Council™ certified paper – one small step in DK's commitment to a sustainable future. Learn more at www.dk.com/uk/information/sustainability

A note from the author

Dr Dean Lomax would like to dedicate this book to pioneering paleontologist, Mary Anning. Through her discoveries, Mary helped pave the way for the science to evolve. Dr Lomax has followed in her footsteps, studying her many ichthyosaur finds and naming the only one after her, *Ichthyosaurus anningae*. He would also like to thank his brother, Scott Lomax, and sister, Julie Boyles, for their support throughout his career.

DK would like to thank:

Soumya Rampal for editorial input; Sakshi Saluja, Ridhima Sikka, and Samrajkumar S for picture research assistance; Polly Goodman for proofreading; Helen Peters for the index; Dilbag Singh for the feature illustrations; Angela Rizza for the pattern and cover illustrations.

The publisher would like to thank the following for their kind permission to reproduce their photographs: (Key: a-above; b-below/bottom; c-centre; f-far; l-left; r-right; t-top)

2 **Alamy Stock Photo:** imageBROKER.com / Daniel Schoenen. 3 **Depositphotos Inc:** Stockdevil_666. 5 **Dreamstime.com:** Tanialerro (bc). 7 **Alamy Stock Photo:** The Natural History Museum (tl). **Dreamstime.com:** Tanialerro (Watercolor Texture). 8 **Dorling Kindersley:** Andy Crawford / Royal Tyrrell Museum of Palaeontology, Alberta, Canada. 9 **123RF.com:** Sayompu Chamnankit (ci). **Alamy Stock Photo:** PjrStudio (tr). **Dorling Kindersley:** National Museum of Wales / Dave King (br). 10 **Alamy Stock Photo:** John Elk III (bl). **NASA:** JPL-Caltech (cr). 11 **Adobe Stock:** Buunature (bl). **Science Photo Library:** Dr. Gilbert S. Grant (crb). 13 **Science Photo Library:** Alan Sirulnikoff. 14 **National Museum of Natural History / Smithsonian Institution:** Han Zeng. 15 **Alamy Stock Photo:** The Natural History Museum. 15–122 **Dreamstime.com:** Tanialerro (Watercolor Texture). 16 **Alamy Stock Photo:** Corbin17. 17 **Science Photo Library:** Science Stock Photography. 19 **Alamy Stock Photo:** The Natural History Museu. 20 **Dreamstime.com:** Oselan. 22 **Alamy Stock Photo:** All Canada Photos / Mark Unrau (bl); The History Collection (t); Design Pics Inc / Michael Melford / Axiom - RF (cr). 23 **Alamy Stock Photo:** Witold Skrypczak (b). **National Museum of Natural History / Smithsonian Institution:** Han Zeng (tl). **Science Photo Library:** Sinclair Stammers (ca). 24 **Alamy Stock Photo:** PB / YB. 25 **Dorling Kindersley:** Natural History Museum, London / Colin Keates (t). 26 **Dorling Kindersley:** Natural History Museum, London / Colin Keates. 27 Deming Wang, Department of Geology, Peking University, Beijing. 28 **Getty Images:** Stone / Ed Reschke. 29 **Alamy Stock Photo:** The Natural History Museum. 30 **Alamy Stock Photo:** The Natural History Museum. 31 Courtesy New Mexico Museum of Natural History & Science/New Mexico Department of Cultural Affairs: Courtesy New Mexico Museum of Natural History & Science / New Mexico Department of Cultural Affairs (b). 32 **Alamy Stock Photo:** Album. 33 **Alamy Stock Photo:** The Natural History Museum (t). 34 Prof. Degan Shu, Northwest University. 35 Prof. John Long, Flinders University. 36 **Alamy Stock Photo:** All Canada Photos / Stephen J. Krasemann. 37 **Alamy Stock Photo:** Nature Picture Library / Doug Perrine. 38 **Alamy Stock Photo:** Tom Stack. 39 **Alamy Stock Photo:** Corbin17. 40 **Dreamstime.com:** Dmitrii Moroz. 41 **Dreamstime.com:** Yezhenliang. 42 **Science Photo Library:** Science Source / Millard H. Sharp. 43 **Dorling Kindersley:** Harry Taylor / University Museum of Zoology, Cambridge (b). 45 **Depositphotos Inc:** Stockdevil_666 46 **Science Photo Library:** Millard H. Sharp. 47 Triebold Paleontology, Inc. 48 Prof. Torsten Scheyer, Paläontologisches Institut. 49 Grzegorz Niedzwiedzki, PhD. 50 naturepl.com: John Cancolosi. 51 **Getty Images / iStock:** Markchentx. 52 Dr Dean Lomax. 53 Dr Dean Lomax. 54 **123RF.com:** Nattawat Khodiaeo (b). **Getty Images:** Corbis Documentary / Walter Geiersperger (t). 55 **Getty Images:** Toronto Star / Bernard Weil (cr). Image Courtesy of the Royal Tyrrell Museum, Drumheller, AB: Sue Sabrowski (t). Xiao-Chun Wu / Canadian Museum Of Nature: Xiao-Chun Wu / Canadian Museum Of Nature (clb). 56 **Alamy Stock Photo:** The Natural History Museum (l). 57 Dr Lida XING. 58 Image Courtesy of the Royal Tyrrell Museum, Drumheller, AB: Sue Sabrowski. 59 **Alamy Stock Photo:** Ron Giling. 61 Jürgen Höflinger, Naturhistorische Gesellschaft Nürnberg. 62 **Getty Images:** AFP / Kazuhiro Nogi. 63 **Dorling Kindersley:** Natural History Museum, London / Colin Keates (t). 64 Louie Psihoyos ©psihoyos.com (c). Prof. Degan Shu, Northwest University: (bl).

65 **Alamy Stock Photo:** Robertharding / Tony Waltham (b). **Science Photo Library:** Dirk Wiersma (t). 66 **Science Photo Library:** Philippe Psaila (t). 67 **Alamy Stock Photo:** Peter Van Evert (b). 68 Kristin Hugo. 69 **Dorling Kindersley:** State Museum of Nature, Stuttgart / Andy Crawford (l). 70 **Alamy Stock Photo:** Mauritius Images GmbH / Steve Vidler (t). 71 **Dorling Kindersley:** Royal Tyrrell Museum of Palaeontology, Alberta, Canada / Andy Crawford (t). 72 Dr. Octávio Mateus. 73 Ryan Hadley. 74 **Dorling Kindersley:** Senckenberg Nature Museum / Andy Crawford (r). 75 **Alamy Stock Photo:** Corbin17. 76 **Science Photo Library:** Millard H. Sharp. 77 **Science Photo Library:** Millard H. Sharp (t). 78 **Alamy Stock Photo:** Fossil & Rock Stock Photos. 79 Photo courtesy of James St. John (Ohio State University at Newark). 80 © Museum of Evolution, Denmark. 81 **Dreamstime.com:** Martina Badini. 82 **Science Photo Library:** Science Source / Millard H. Sharp. 83 **Alamy Stock Photo:** ZUMA Press, Inc. / Kayte Deioma. 84 **Getty Images / iStock:** Crazytang (t). 85 **Getty Images:** AFP / Saul Loeb. 86 **Dorling Kindersley:** Royal Tyrrell Museum of Palaeontology, Alberta, Canada / Andy Crawford. 87 **Dorling Kindersley:** Oxford Museum of Natural History / Gary Ombler (t). 89 **Alamy Stock Photo:** Rick Rudnicki. 90 Tarina Peterson. 91 **Alamy Stock Photo:** Roland Bouvier (b). 92 Daniel Ksepka: © Departamento de Paleontologia de Vertebrados, Museo de Historia. 93 **National Museum of Natural History / Smithsonian Institution.** 94 **Alamy Stock Photo:** Dave Stamboulis (b). 95 **Science Photo Library:** Millard H. Sharp. 96 Edwin Cadena, Universidad del Rosario. 97 **Alamy Stock Photo:** Martin Shields (l). 98 **Alamy Stock Photo:** SuperStock / RGB Ventures / Fred Hirschmann (br). **Dreamstime.com:** Wirestock (cl). 99 **Alamy Stock Photo:** Werner Dieterich (tr). **Getty Images:** Universal Images Group / Wild Horizon (a). **Shutterstock.com:** James Kirkikis (b). 100 **Alamy Stock Photo:** Corbin17. 101 **Dorling Kindersley:** Natural History Museum, London / Colin Keates. 102 **Alamy Stock Photo:** Phil Degginger. 103 California Academy of Sciences: from www.antweb.org / Photographer: Ute Kiel / SMFMEI00998 Titanomyrma gigantea. 104 **Alamy Stock Photo:** Minden Pictures / Albert Lleal. 106 Dr. Xiaoming Wang, Natural History Museum of Los Angeles. 107 **Science Photo Library:** Millard H. Sharp (b). 108 **Alamy Stock Photo:** Roberto Nistri (t). 109 **Shutterstock.com:** Melnikov Dmitriy. 110 **Alamy Stock Photo:** Sabena Jane Blackbird (b). 111 **Dorling Kindersley:** Natural History Museum, London / Colin Keates. 112 Dr Dean Lomax. 113 **Alamy Stock Photo:** Aaron Parker. 114 Alison Schwabe. 115 **Alamy Stock Photo:** Q-Images. 116 **Alamy Stock Photo:** The Natural History Museum. 117 **Dorling Kindersley:** Oxford Museum of Natural History / Gary Ombler. 118 **GNS Science:** Wendy St George, GNS Science (cr). Courtesy of the NC Museum of Natural Sciences: (bl). 119 **Alamy Stock Photo:** Lou Linwei (bl). Dr. Karen Chin: Casey Cass / University of Colorado Boulder (t). Dr Dean Lomax: (cr). 120 **Science Photo Library:** VW Pics / Jon G. Fulle (b). 121 **Alamy Stock Photo:** Jon G. Fuller / VWPics (tl). **Getty Images:** China News Service (br). **Science Photo Library:** Marco Ansaloni (cr). 122 **Alamy Stock Photo:** Rob Judges Scienc (bl). **Dreamstime.com:** Milosluz (t); Antonio Ribeiro (cra). 123 **Alamy Stock Photo:** Wavebreak Media ltd / PH73 (b).

Cover images: *Front:* **Depositphotos Inc:** Stockdevil_666; *Back:* **Alamy Stock Photo:** All Canada Photos / Stephen J. Krasemann tl, PjrStudio tc; *Spine:* **Depositphotos Inc:** Stockdevil_666